IT'S AN ACT OF HILARITY!

Hundreds of jokes, limericks, wisecracks and one-liners will keep you up nights laughing! No one escapes—feminists, dudes, seniors, marrieds, and more, more, *more*! You'll scream with rib-tickling ecstasy!

Larry Wilde has poked fun at pets, politicians, parents, professions, and everything from ethnics to golfnicks. Now he's gone from virgins to sex maniacs to *more* sex maniacs to

THE LAST OFFICIAL
SEX MANIACS JOKE BOOK

The *Last* Official Sex Maniacs Joke Book

Larry Wilde

Illustrated by Ron Wing

BANTAM BOOKS
TORONTO · NEW YORK · LONDON · SYDNEY · AUCKLAND

THE *LAST* OFFICIAL SEX MANIACS JOKE BOOK
A BANTAM BOOK 0 553 22919 2

First publication in Great Britain

PRINTING HISTORY
Bantam edition published 1986

Copyright © 1982 by Larry Wilde
Illustrations copyright © 1982 by Ron Wing

This book is set in Plantin 9 pt.

Bantam Books are published by Transworld Publishers Ltd.,
61-63 Uxbridge Road, Ealing, London W5 5SA,
in Australia by Transworld Publishers (Aust.) Pty. Ltd.,
15-23 Helles Avenue, Moorbank, NSW 2170, and in New
Zealand by Transworld Publishers (N.Z.) Ltd., Cnr. Moselle
and Waipareira Avenues, Henderson, Auckland.

Printed and bound in Great Britain by
Cox & Wyman Ltd, Reading

To Mort Fleischmann, last
of the truly great sex maniacs

CONTENTS

Bawdy Baubles

Steve stalked into the drugstore on Monday morning and shouted at the manager, "Friday night, I came in here and bought a gross of condoms. Later, I counted them and found five missing."

"Sorry to have ruined your weekend, sir," said the manager.

* * *

1

Jacques was dining with his fiancée. "Before we get married," he purred, "I want to confess some affairs I've had in the past."

"But you told me all about those a couple of weeks ago," replied the girl.

"Yes, *ma chérie*," he explained, "but that was a couple of weeks ago."

*   *   *

What can a jelly bean do that a man can't do?

Come in eight delicious colors.

*   *   *

A pianist in Reno, Nevada,
Plays rinky-tink numbers like "Jada"
    But once she gets screwed,
    It changes her mood
To pieces like Moonlight Sonata!

*   *   *

Sandy Shaw, the Oh Dawn! executive secretary, sent in this snappy smiler:

Why is it bad to be an egg?

You get laid once, eaten once, it takes ten minutes to get hard, and you come in a box with eleven others.

*   *   *

Dennis and Agatha were arguing in their bedroom. "Take off my dress!" she said. "Now take off my bra! Now take off my pantyhose! Now take off my girdle!"

Then she said, "Don't ever let me catch you wearing my clothes again!"

* * *

"I call my girl 'Rowboat.' "

"But that's ridiculous. A rowboat is a big thing with a pointed nose and a flat bottom."

"That's my girl."

* * *

Lil: Yipe! I've been geesed.
Wes: You mean "goosed."
Lil: I mean "geesed." I can tell when you use two fingers.

* * *

What kind of a bee makes milk?
A boobie.

* * *

Did you hear about the new candy bar containing a birth control pill?
They say it's inconceivably delicious.

3

Carlson, on vacation in Egypt, was crossing the desert astride a camel when suddenly the animal stopped and would not move. Carlson got down and tried pushing, to no avail. A woman driving by in a jeep stopped and asked, "What's the problem?"

"My camel won't move," he replied.

The woman reached down underneath the camel, and in a flash the camel took off like a bolt of lightning.

"What did you do?" asked the tourist.

"I just reached between his legs and tickled his testicles."

Carlson quickly dropped his pants and said, "You better start tickling mine. I gotta go catch him."

ULTIMATE REJECTION

When you're masturbating and your hand falls asleep.

* * *

Prescott was quite shy. He bought a lady friend a pair of gloves as a birthday present and wrote a note to be sent along with them:

"I sure hope you like these. I noticed on our last few dates that you weren't wearing any. They are reversible, so if you get them soiled, you can wear them inside out and thereby wear them longer without having to wash them. I'm real sorry I can't be there at your party to watch your smiling face as you try them on."

Prescott left the note with the saleslady, who sent it off with the wrong package: a pair of silk panties.

* * *

What is the difference between dark and hard?

It can stay dark all night long.

* * *

Remember the girl on top of the hill
Who won't put out but her sister will?
Her sister did and forgot the pill . . .
Now she's on her way to the *hospitill*!

* * *

Rick and Corrine met at a deserted California nude beach. They were strolling near the water's edge when Rick said, "Don't look now, but I think I'm falling in love with you."

* * *

What is the similarity between a virgin and a hemophiliac?
One prick and it's all over.

* * *

How does a cub scout become a boy scout?
He has to eat two brownies.

* * *

BROWNIE POINTS

Boobs on a girl scout

* * *
7

What do a soy bean hamburger and a dildo have in common?

They're both meat substitutes.

* * *

Barbara and Jim were roommates. One night she walked in on Jim while he was playing with himself. "Hey," said Barbara, "what're you doing?"

"I'm trying to jump start a vibrator," he replied.

* * *

Withdrawal, according to Freud,
Is a very good thing to avoid.
    If practiced each day,
    Your balls will decay
To the size of a small adenoid.

* * *

Doctor: What seems to be your problem?
Lenora: Every time I sneeze, I feel sexy.
Doctor: What have you been taking for it?
Lenora: Snuff.

* * *

* * *

Gary and Erika, adjusting their clothes after a back-seat quickie: "Gosh," said Gary, "if I had known you were still a virgin, I'd have taken more time."

"Well," she rejoined, "if I had known you had more time, I'd have taken off my pantyhose."

* * *

How can you tell a guy is getting older?

When he keeps asking at a group sex party, "What? My turn again?"

* * *

The Seven Dwarfs were sitting around one night having a few brews. "Hey," said Grumpy, "any of you guys ever see Snow White in the nude?"

"Naw," they all replied.

"Why don't we look through her window, then," suggested Grumpy.

The seven little men climbed on each other's shoulders, with Doc on top peering through Snow White's window. "She's taking off her dress," reported Doc.

Below him, Grumpy repeated, "She's taking off her dress."

"She's taking off her dress," said Dopey.

"Taking off her dress," said Sneezy.

Each dwarf passed the word down to the one below him.

Up at the top, looking through the window, Doc announced, "She's taking off her bra."

"Taking off her bra."

"Taking off her bra." The words filtered all the way down.

"Hey," said Doc at the top, "great boobs."

"Big boobs." said Grumpy.

"Big boobs," etc., etc.

Then Doc spoke again. "She's taking off her panties. She's completely naked."

"Taking off panties. She's naked."

"Taking off panties. She's naked." All the way to the bottom.

"Hold it," said Doc. "Someone's coming!"

"Someone's coming," repeated Grumpy.

"Me, too. . . ."

"Me, too. . . ."

". . . . ."

* * *

TRAVEL NEWS

While in London, Jennifer bicycled from one end of the city to the other over the roughest cobblestone streets. It's doubtful if she'll ever come that way again.

* * *

Bobbi Bressee, the glamorous TV actress, tells about the twins Jeffrey and Adam. The two boys hadn't seen each other in years when they ran into each other accidentally at a party. "You remember me," said Jeffrey. "I used to be your womb mate."

* * *

"Had any real kicks lately?"
"Last weekend, I went to a wild, crazy porno movie. Even the cashier was nude."

12

* * *

There was a young pessimist Grotton
Who wished he had ne'er been begotten,
    Nor would he have been,
    But the rubber was thin,
And right at the tip it was rotten.

* * *

Did you hear about the nearsighted girl who can't tell her friends until they're right on top of her?

* * *

SMART ASS

A guy who can sit on an ice cream cone and tell you what flavor it is

* * *

Did you hear about the fellow who slept with his sister-in-law?
He had it in for his brother.

13

* * *

Aretha: Do you love me still?
Eugene: I might if you stayed still long enough.

* * *

If a light sleeper sleeps with a light on, does a hard sleeper sleep with a window open?

* * *

"Is it in?" he asked.
"Yes," she said.
"Does it hurt?" he asked.
"No," she said.
So he sold her a new pair of shoes.

* * *

"You unattached?"
"No. Just put together sloppy."

* * *

What did the right tit say to the left tit?
We better stop hanging so low or they'll think we're nuts.

* * *

Fenton walked into the pharmacy and found his favorite clerk.

"I've got crabs," Fenton whispered. "I need something to get rid of them. Something new."

"Well," said the clerk, "try this. It's called Beast-Away, and it costs three dollars a bottle."

"Does it kill crabs?"

"No, but it's fluorescent so you can pick them out in the dark."

* * *

A girl named Alice in Dallas
Had never felt of a phallus.
    She remained virgo intacto
    Because, ipso facto,
No phallus in Dallas fit Alice.

* * *

Did you hear about the latest sex poll? Two hundred men were asked their opinions on women's thighs.

One percent said they preferred thin thighs.

One percent said they preferred fat thighs.

The other 98 percent said they preferred something in between.

* * *

Pete strolled into a Seattle night spot and sat down at the bar. After a couple of Scotches, he noticed this sign over the bar:

GIRLS NOT ALLOWED
TO SMOKE AT THE
COCKTAIL BAR

Pete called over the barkeep and asked, "What's the reason for that?"

"Well," explained the bartender, "after they have a few drinks, they get careless with their butts."

17

Why does Miss Piggy douche with vinegar and water?

Because Kermit likes sweet and sour pork.

* * *

Steven and Mark walked into a San Francisco hotel lounge and took seats at the bar.

"What'll you have?" asked the bartender.

"Make mine a rum punch," said Mark.

"Rum punch," repeated the barkeep. "What about the fruit?"

"Oh, he doesn't drink."

* * *

While sitting in a Philadelphia cocktail lounge, Matson noticed the bartender mixing an exotic drink. "What's that?" he asked.

"I call this a brandy dandy," replied the barkeep.

"What's in it?"

"Sugar, milk, and brandy," said the bartender.

"Is it good?" asked Matson.

"Sure," said the bartender. "The sugar gives you pep; the milk gives you energy."

"And the brandy?"

"Ideas about what to do with all that pep and energy."

18

What has eight legs and a cherry?
Four barmaids and a Manhattan.

* * *

What's the similarity between a penis and Rubik's cube?
The longer you play with it the harder it gets.

* * *

There was a cute waitress named Hoople
Whose bosom was triple, not duple.
    She had one removed,
    But it grew back improved.
At present, Miss Hoople's quadruple.

* * *

What would you get if you crossed a rooster with an owl?
A cock that stays up all night.

* * *

Did you hear about the medical researcher who was trying to cross a donkey with an onion?
Most of the time he got onions with long ears, but every so often he would get a piece of ass that made his eyes water.

* * *

LADIES' ROOM GRAFFITI

Squatters' writes

* * *

What do you get when you cross a rooster with peanut butter?

A cock that sticks to the roof of your mouth.

* * *

What's the difference between a donkey, an egg, and sex?

You can beat a donkey. You can beat an egg. But you can't beat sex.

* * *

Garrick walked into a Ft. Worth restaurant and noticed that the waitresses were all wearing new uniforms. Across the left breast pocket on each uniform, the girls' names were embroidered. One of the waitresses faced him and said, "How do you like it?"

"Great!" he replied. "But what're you gonna name the other one?"

* * *

Can you think of three two-letter words meaning "small"?
Is it in?

* * *

RAIN REFRAIN

She was only the weatherman's daughter, but she could love up a storm.

* * *

When is a girl a virgin?
One time out of twenty!

* * *

Tony Zavarelli, Bantam's super bookseller, gets howls with this happy dash of high jinks:

Science has now established that plants, like people, respond to "sweet talk." Norton, the owner of a New Orleans nursery, noticed that more and more of the people who entered his establishment talked gently to the various plants.

One day, a man walked in scowling and seemed to be muttering to the plants. Norton approached the stranger and heard him using foul language. He called the police and the man was arrested. The charge? Making obscene fern calls!

21

Milwaukee Millie developed a reputation for exuberant lovemaking. Here was a woman who enjoyed sex seven days a week.

One afternoon, the Wisconsin nympho sat in the physician's examination room and described her ailments. When she had itemized all her symptoms, the doctor finally spoke. "All right, just take your clothes off and lie down on this table."

"What!" exclaimed Millie. "Without a martini first?"

Did you hear about the new diaphragm of transparent plastic?

It gives you a womb with a view.

* * *

What do you give to the incurable romantic?

Penicillin.

* * *

SPERM-BANK DEPOSITS

Merchants' semen

* * *

Nancy, a doctor's receptionist, truly flipped over Paul Newman and Robert Redford. She decided to get a picture of her two heroes tattooed on her thighs. Nancy didn't earn much money, so she went to Thompson's tattoo parlor, the cheapest in town.

The unshaved artist tattooed Paul Newman's face on Nancy's right inside thigh and Robert Redford on her left.

When the painful task was over, she took a look in the mirror and was horrified. "These faces don't look anything like Paul Newman or Robert Redford!" she cried.

"Ah, lady, sure they do," protested the artist.

"They're awful!" raved the receptionist.

"No, they're not," said the tattooer. "I'll go get a stranger off the street and ask him his opinion. OK?"

She agreed. Thompson went out on the street and woke up a passed-out wino. He offered him a pint to come in and tell the girl that the pictures on her legs looked like Paul Newman and Robert Redford.

The drunk approached the spread-eagled girl and examined the work.

"Now my good man," said the tattoo artist, "who do those faces remind you of?"

"The one on the left looksh like Paul Newman, and the one on the right looksh like Robert Redford," said the swaying wino, "and I'd say the one in the middle is either Willy Nelson or Gentle Ben."

* * *

A sea captain bought an inflatable rubber woman in a Hong Kong sex shop and kept it hidden in his quarters. One day, the captain accidentally left it inflated on his bunk, and when he was called to the bridge during a storm, the first mate used it.

Six months later, the captain returned to the sex shop. "How you like rubber lady?" asked the owner. "Was she realistic?"

"I'll say she was," answered the captain. "So realistic she gave me the clap."

* * *

FUNERAL DIRECTOR'S DITTY

She was only a mortician's daughter, but she sure could put a stiff in her box.

* * *

What's the best thing that comes out of a penis when you kiss it?
The wrinkles.

Female Funnies

Pauline and Frances, two supersexy ladies, were chatting at a bar. "Then what happened?" asked Pauline.

"Well," replied Frances, "after he called me a nymphomaniac, I told him to get the hell out of my bed and to take his two buddies with him!"

* * *

Yvonne arrived at the hardware store holding a hinge in her hand and approached the clerk. "Can I give you a screw for that hinge?" he asked.

"No," said Yvonne, "but I'll give you a blow job for that electric toaster."

* * *

Abbie and Berta had married at the same time and were reminiscing about their honeymoon.

"What do you remember most about yours?" asked Abbie.

"It was when Alex took me in his arms on the first night in Niagara Falls and whispered, 'Darling, at last we're one.' "

"I also had my biggest thrill on the first night of the honeymoon," said Berta. "Richard and I were walking across the hotel lobby when I spotted the house detective standing under a palm tree. What a thrill it was thumbing my nose at him!"

* * *

A young Polish girl named Swoboda
Had built a new kind of pagoda.
    The walls of its halls
    Were hung with the balls
And the tools of the fools that bestrode her.

Richie Benson, the brilliant Seattle watercolor artist, chuckles over this cajoler:

Finlay, a Madison Avenue exec, went to a Greenwich Village cocktail party. He struck up a conversation with a pretty model and soon began complaining about his wife's constant visits to her mother. "She's away again tonight," said Finlay. "What would you do if you were in my place?"

"Well, honey," cooed the model, "let's go over to your place and I'll show you."

* * *

Did you hear about the girl who was fired from her job in a sperm bank after she became pregnant?

They discovered she'd been embezzling.

* * *

The nosy neighbor approached the expectant mother next door and asked her, "Are you going to have a baby, Emma?"

Smiling sweetly, the young woman replied, "Oh, no! I'm just carrying this for a friend."

* * *

* * *

Marty the milkman was having intercourse with Maria the Mexican maid standing up against the door in the hall of a La Jolla home. After he finished, Marty noticed that she was still wiggling and writhing. "Whatsa matter, honey?" he asked. "Didn't I satisfy you?"

"Oh, sure," she replied. "But I no can get dee damn doorknob out!"

* * *

Marianne had just bought some lingerie at Bloomingdale's. "I'd like to get the sentence 'If you can read this, you are too damn close' embroidered on the panties," she said to the clerk.

"Yes, madam," the saleswoman replied. "I'm sure that can be done. Do you want block or script letters?"

"Braille," said Marianne.

* * *

Ernie stopped his Eldorado and said to the girl hitchhiker, "If I give you a ride, what's in it for me?"

She replied, "Dust. I've been walking all day."

* * *

There was a hot girl from Del Mar
Who screwed all both from near and
from far.
When asked to explain,
She replied with disdain,
"I'm trying to buy me a car."

* * *

"Loraine is really a linguist."
"Why?"
"She's the only girl I know who can
speak English and French at the same time."

* * *

Nick joined a nudist camp, and on the
very first day he suddenly found himself
sporting an erection. Thinking quickly, he
grabbed a banana peel from a nearby trash
basket, sheathed the organ, and stood there
quite innocently.

Just then, a well-endowed young blonde
camper sashayed up to him. "Hey, there,
big fella." She smiled. "How'd you like to
put that thing in a split?"

* * *

BIKINI BOTTOM

A gash mask

31

Jan Dwyer, the incomparable California carpenter, came up with this country cutie:

Oliver and Martha were walking back from town along a deserted road. Oliver carried a large bucket, a chicken, and a broom and was leading a goat. They strolled silently until they reached a secluded spot.

"I'm afraid, walking along with you," said Martha, "you might try to take advantage of me."

"But how could I?" asked the farm boy. "Look at the things I'm carryin' and the goat I'm leadin'."

"Well," said Martha, "you could stick that broom handle in the ground, tie the goat to it, then put the chicken on the ground under the bucket, couldn't you?"

32

33

Nita, Peggy, and Larissa, three Detroit stenos, were chatting during a coffee break. The general subject was men, specifically what kind of man they'd prefer being shipwrecked with on a desert island.

"I'd want a fellow who was a wonderful conversationalist," said Nita.

"That would be nice," said Peggy, "but I'd rather have a guy who knew how to hunt and could cook the things he caught."

"Me," said Larissa, "I'd settle for a good obstetrician."

* * *

Phillip and Hilda, sitting next to each other on a train, were conversing amiably when they passed a bull mounting a cow in the field.

"How does he know she wants it?" asked Hilda.

Phillip explained that it was all done by the sense of smell, that during a certain period of the year, the instincts are sharpened.

They rode along in silence until parting at their station, when Hilda quipped, "So long. Come up and see me sometime when you haven't got that cold in your head!"

* * *

Did you hear about this gal who combined making love and playing tennis?

She served in bed.

* * *

Betty didn't mind going on the blind date, but right from the outset, it was a fiasco. The evening got progressively worse, and the self-proclaimed Romeo from the Bronx was too egotistical to realize it. The moment of truth came in a cocktail-lounge booth as he clutched Betty's thigh and whispered, "Hey, doll, how about us going to my pad so I can slip you nine inches?"

"You know," said the girl, "I really don't think you could get it up three times in a row."

* * *

"What about it, honey? C'mon. What do you say? Huh? How's about it?"

"Stop asking me and get started or I'll put my clothes on and go home."

* * *

"I'd like you to kiss me," she said.

"Between my toes . . . please bend your head.

Not there . . . oh, no, no!

It tickles me so . . .

Between the two big ones, instead!"

Marion left Boston for her first trip to England. One night while dancing with a dapper Englishman, her brooch became unfastened and slid down inside her dress.

She told her escort about it and asked him to retrieve the lost article. Somewhat embarrassed but determined to please, he reached cautiously down the back of her gown. After a moment, he said, "Awfully sorry, but I can't seem to locate it."

"Try farther down," suggested the Bostonian. He did, beginning to blush. Still no brooch. "Down still farther," she ordered.

The Englishman noticed that he was being watched by every couple on the dance floor. He blushed a deep purple and whispered, "I feel a perfect ass."

"Never mind that!" she snapped. "Just get the brooch!"

Allison was confiding in her older, and wiser, sister about what happened the previous evening. "We went to a movie, then to a nice restaurant, and then I went up to his apartment for a few drinks. Did I do wrong?"

"Don't you remember?"

* * *

BUMPER STICKER

Overpopulation is everybody's *baby*.

* * *

Howard was sleeping overnight with Norma, the airline stewardess, when he suddenly began to make strange noises.

She woke him and he explained, "I dreamt I was dangling over the edge of a precipice, my fingers desperately entwined in a bush I had grabbed for support."

"You're safe," whispered Norma. "So relax."

"I'll be all right now," muttered Howard. "You go back to sleep, honey."

"I will," said the stew, "if you'll just let go of the bush."

* * *

*   *   *

Eunice: When I ask my date to hook up
my dress in the back, he fumbles
around like he was all thumbs.

Dottie: He's just like all men. They sure
don't have any trouble when it
comes to taking them off!

*   *   *

Rowena, a Brooklyn steno, was vacationing at a Virginia farmhouse. On Satur-
day night, at the barn dance, she drank a
little too much and passed out. The boys
laid her in a cow stall to sleep it off. Sometime later, Cora the cow went into the same
stall.

Next morning, a farm hand came out
and tried to pull the slumbering Rowena out
from under the udders so he could milk.

"Go away, you hick!" shouted the
Brooklyn gal. "I've got four guys halfway
limp, and I'll drain 'em dry if it takes
forever!"

*   *   *

Felicia was brought up in a strict religious environment and had remained a virgin. But she suffered from acute nervousness due to repressed desires and finally decided to visit Dr. Roden, a well-known Park Avenue psychiatrist.

After twenty minutes of questioning the voluptuous virgin, Roden lost all his professional objectivity. "Take off your clothes," he ordered, scarcely able to disguise the lust in his voice. "Now lie down on this couch. Now close your eyes and very slowly spell the word 'bedroom.'"

She began, "B . . . E . . . D . . . R . . . Oh! . . . Ohhh . . . Mmmmmmmmmmmm mmmmmmmmmm."

She was cured.

Julie came home one day and told her mother she was pregnant. "My God!" exclaimed the mother. "How could this happen? When did it happen? Who's the father?"

"I don't know," replied the girl. "I was drunk. It happened at a surprise party at the beach. And I don't know who the father is. There were eight of them!"

* * *

Ann: One more drink could make me love you.
Hal: Whatssat?
Ann: I said, one more drink could make me . . .

* * *

GENTLEMANLY

The way a man treats a woman he hasn't got enough from yet

* * *

A redhead with features cherubic
Was famed for her area pubic.
　　When they asked her its size,
　　She replied in surprise,
"Are you speaking of square feet or cubic?"

42

Theo rushed in to his fiancée's bedroom and tried to rape her. She began berating him angrily.

"Two words," he pleaded. "Let me say two words!"

After exhausting her vocabulary of insults, she finally said, "All right, what's your two words, you dirty bum!"

"Let go!"

* * *

Miss Lenczewski, the waitress, picked up a strong, handsome steelworker at the local cocktail lounge. Later, they went to her apartment. Next morning at breakfast, her date found nothing on his plate but a head of lettuce.

"What's this?" he asked.

"I just wanted to see if you eat like a rabbit, too!" said the Polish girl.

* * *

The couple were hugging and kissing in the darkened living room. "What are you thinking about?" whispered Monica.

"The same thing you are!" said Keefe, panting.

"Then I'll race you to the refrigerator!" shouted the girl.

* * *

Two Polish women met at the super-market.

"Did you hear about Angelica? She's getting married."

"Married? I didn't even know she was pregnant!"

* * *

Claudia was telling her mother about the great time she had at the Pennsylvania resort. "I met this guy in the recreation hall, and we played Ping Pong for hours. What fun!"

"Why," remarked the mother, "I didn't know you liked Ping Pong."

"I do now," said Claudia. "I'd hit the ball the wrong way, and we'd both go after it under the table. Then he'd hit the ball wrong, and we'd both go after it under the table. We played all night. It was wonderful."

"But I don't understand," said her mother. "Where does the fun come in?"

"Under the table, silly."

* * *

Janice met her friend Harriet at a wild party. "How's it goin'?" asked Janice.

"If I'm not in bed by ten o'clock," said Harriet, "I'm going home."

44

FILIBUSTER

A falsie manufacturer

* * *

Evangeline, an Indiana milkmaid, entered a contest for the best poem about condensed milk. She won first prize, but the verse was never broadcast on the radio. Here's why:

There's a red carnation on the can
'Cause it's the best milk in the land.
No tits to twitch,
No chips to pitch,
Just punch two holes in the sonuvabitch!

* * *

Cinderella was getting ready to go to the ball. "Remember now," said the good fairy, "if you're not home by midnight, your twat will turn into a pumpkin."

Cinderella went to the ball, met the prince, and they had a beautiful evening. While they were dancing, Cinderella looked at her watch and exclaimed, "Oh, my, it's three minutes to midnight. I've got to go."

"But you can't," said the prince. "I don't even know your name."

"I'm Cinderella. Who are you?"

"I'm Peter, Peter, pumpkin eater."

"I can stay another five minutes." said Cindy.

Arlene, a Broadway showgirl, was built like a brick chicken house. When summer arrived, she spent almost all of her time on the roof of her hotel tanning her magnificent bod.

She wore a bathing suit the first day, but on the second she felt quite brave, and she slipped out of it for an overall tan. Suddenly, Arlene heard footsteps coming up the stairs. She was lying on her stomach, so she pulled a towel over her gorgeous buns and continued to recline as before.

"Excuse me," said the manager, "the hotel doesn't mind you sunning on the roof, but could you wear a bathing suit like you did yesterday."

"Why?" asked the showgirl. "No one can see me up here. Besides, I'm covered with a towel."

"Not exactly," he replied. "You're lying on the dining-room skylight."

* * *

Dave met Brandy, a brassiere model, at a party. They hit it off and were spending the weekend together. On the first afternoon, the egotistical stud asked his more than willing shack mate, "On a scale of one to ten, how would you rate my performance?"

"Three," replied the girl. "But you have seven more chances to get a perfect score."

* * *

Christine, a pretty Hollywood starlet, was in the powder room of a fashionable Beverly Hills restaurant. One of her envious acquaintances asked, "Darling, how did you get that lovely mink?"

Another woman said, "Chris, how did you manage that fantastic sports car?"

A third woman queried, "Christine, how could you afford those diamonds?"

"Darlings," she responded, "I simply had another deposit made in my bank account."

Suddenly, Christine's cigarette dropped into her lap and her flimsy dress burst into flames. "Help, help!" yelled one of the women. "The bank's on fire!"

* * *

Margaret, an attractive blonde, went to a bank every Friday and deposited $10,000. Benton, the bank president, was fascinated by the sums she was depositing and one Friday invited her into his office.

"I'm sorry for being so curious," he said, "but ten thousand dollars is a lot of money to deposit each and every week. May I ask what you do for a living?"

"I'm a gambler. I make my money on unusual bets. As an example—if you'll excuse me for being so crude—I'll bet you ten thousand dollars that by next Friday your balls will be square."

Benton chuckled but quickly agreed. He went to the doctor each day. He checked his scrotum every morning and night. Soon Friday arrived, and so did Margaret and her lawyer.

They went into the banker's office. "I believe I win, young lady," said Benton.

"Well, let's see."

The president dropped his pants, pulled down his underwear, and Margaret began fingering his testicles. The lawyer fainted.

"You do win," said Margaret. "Here's your money."

"What happened to your lawyer?"

"Nothing. I bet him twenty thousand dollars I'd have my banker by the balls on Friday."

* * *

PRUDE

*A female who doesn't drink,
doesn't smoke, and only curses
when it slips out*

* * *

Dodie and Andrea were gossiping about a mutual friend. "Did you know Magda went to a masquerade ball in the nude?"

"What was that supposed to mean?"

"She said she represented an unfurnished apartment, ready for a bachelor to move in."

Dude Dillies

Monroe, the macho superstud, just returned from his first visit to a nudist camp. "How'd you like it?" asked a buddy.

"Well," said Monroe, "the first three days were the hardest."

* * *

Sanders and Wilson, two Chicago ad execs, met in the elevator. "How come your secretary doesn't wear underpants?" asked Sanders.

"How do you know she doesn't?" inquired Wilson.

"A little birdie told me," said Sanders. "A goose to be exact."

51

* * *

PHIL'S PHILOSOPHY

Discovering a virgin nowadays is very much like finding a parking space in the city. There are mighty few left, and just when you think you've spotted a good one, some S.O.B. cuts in ahead of you.

* * *

There was a young fellow named Pete
Who was gentle and shy and discreet;
But with his first woman
He became quite inhuman
And constantly roared for fresh meat.

* * *

At a Laguna Beach swingers' party, the orgy was going full blast. Neal couldn't get a stuck-up sexpot to participate. "What's the matter," muttered the girl, "are you still trying to line up your first piece?"

"No, I've had lots, and they all said they liked it," said the stud. "But I was hoping you could give me a *professional* opinion."

* * *

Did you hear about the company president who moved into his lavish new office, then had his interior designer on the carpet because she'd forgotten to include a couch?

* * *

Letitia lay naked on the motel bed observing Hugo, the guy who picked her up. As she watched, several thoughts went through her mind: *he wasn't much on the dance floor. He's probably underhung. I can't imagine why he handed me this felt-tip pen . . . this dude's probably got something kinky in mind. . . .*

Suddenly, Letitia's eyes widened. When the fellow pulled off his shorts, she saw the extent of his manhood and almost fainted. Then he spoke. "I'll take that pen now, baby. For your sake, I think I should draw the line somewhere."

* * *

DUDE DIRECTIVE

Men and women continually fight,
And the women win . . . it's quite a sight.
But when it's over and they stop,
It's often the man who comes out on top!

Kirby met Cheryl at a wedding reception. Later that night, they had their own celebration in her pad. When they finished, Kirby said, "You're very good."

"I wish I could say the same for you." Cheryl yawned.

"You could" came the reply, "if you were as big a liar as I am!"

* * *

"What kind of a lover is Jerome?"

"Are you kidding? This guy's gone down on everything but the *Titanic*!"

* * *

Adele and Noah got engaged and went to the doctor for premarital examinations. On his lunch hour, Noah stopped at the doctor's office to obtain the results.

"I'm afraid that I have both bad and good news for you," said the M.D. "The bad news is that your fiancée has gonorrhea."

"That's terrible!" moaned Noah. "And what's the good news?"

"She didn't get it from you!"

* * *

"How'd you like being at that nudist wedding?"

"Not bad. I came within an inch of being best man."

* * *

Gabe, a Laramie carpenter, went to a singles' dance and spotted a very pretty blonde sitting at a corner table by herself. He wandered over and asked her to dance.

"I'd love to," said the girl, "but I don't have any arms or legs."

Gabe was shocked for a moment, but he looked at her closely and saw that she was, in fact, armless and legless. They talked for an hour and then he asked, "Can I drive you home?" She agreed.

After driving a few miles outside the city, he pulled the car over to the side of a deserted road. Soon they were kissing like crazy.

"Slip this coat hanger under my dress," said the girl, "and move it to my shoulders so the hook comes out behind my head. Hook me onto the telephone pole and we can get it on."

He did, and they made it like mad.

Later, when they arrived at her house, he carried her inside. Gabe took the girl's father aside and said, "I'm real sorry about this," and told him what happened.

"Don't feel bad," said the father. "I should be thanking you—most guys just leave her hanging out on the telephone pole."

Guido and Joanna were making love on the beach one night. "Is it in?" asked Guido.

"No," said Joanna, "it's in the sand."

"Now is it in?"

"Oh, yes!"

A minute later, Guido said, "I think I'll try it in the sand again!"

A glutted debauchee named Bloom
Lured beauteous maids to his room,
    Where, after he'd strip 'em,
    He'd generally whip 'em
With a bundle of twigs or a broom.

* * *

Sawyer checked into a hotel. "For ten dollars extra," said the clerk, "you can have O.T.O."

"What's OTO?"

"Overlooking the ocean!"

"OK," said Sawyer.

"For five dollars extra, you can have B.I.B."

"What's that?"

"Breakfast in bed!"

"OK."

The next morning, the maid came in with his breakfast. "F.U.C.K.," said Sawyer.

The maid rushed out of the room and went down and complained to the desk clerk. He walked into Sawyer's room and exclaimed, "What's the idea of insulting the maid with that foul language!"

"What're you talkin' about?" said Sawyer. "All I said was F.U.C.K."

"Well, that's dirty enough!"

"But all that means is First U Could've Knocked."

HANKY

*A small square piece of cloth
used for wiping off the PANKY*

* * *

There once was a fellow named Abbott
Who made love to girls as a habit;
    But he ran for the door
    When one asked for more
And exclaimed, "I'm a man, not a
rabbit."

* * *

Have you heard about the new drug
made of LSD, Spanish fly, and Epsom salts?
    It's for those who enjoy a trip but don't
care whether they're coming or going.

* * *

Chuck and Hank, the town's biggest
studs, were out fishing in a boat when it
started to leak. Chuck hopped into the water
and tried to plug up the hole. After trying in
vain, he said, "Dammit, I can't seem to
find the hole under water."
    "That's odd," said Hank, "you wouldn't
have any trouble if it had hair around it!"

* * *

Gerald Siegel, the handsome Hollywood actor, offered this little hunk:

Baker was walking along the Santa Monica beach early one Sunday morning when his foot landed on a hard metal object. Baker pulled it out of the sand and discovered it was a lamp. He rubbed it, and out came a genie.

"Oh, this is just a dream!" cried Baker.

"No, master. It is real," said the genie. "Because you have released me, I will give you three wishes. You may have anything you want, but your worst enemy will have double!"

"Okay," said Baker. "I want five million dollars."

"You shall have it. And your worst enemy will have ten million."

"I want one hundred gorgeous girls to be at my beck and call twenty-four hours a day."

"Done. And your enemy shall have two hundred girls," said the genie. "And now what is your third wish?"

"Cut off my left nut!"

61

After Sterling entertained the circus performer with food and drink, she felt kind of obligated. "Listen," she said, "I have Santa Claus tattooed on my stomach. Would you like to feel his beard?"

"Sure," said Sterling. But when he took her up on the invitation, she yelled, "Hey, I didn't say you could put your finger in his mouth!"

* * *

OPPORTUNIST

A dude who rapes a girl in a public library

* * *

At a country dance, Cindy became excited by the man's extremely large erection pressing against her body and hastily agreed to go to bed with him.

In the bedroom, she observed him taking a broom handle out of his pants pocket.

"Hey!" cried Cindy. "I thought that was your prick!"

"No, ma'am, that's my decoy!"

* * *

Lloyd, Mort, and Stash were lost in the wilds of northern Nevada. They had been wandering around for six days in desperation.

"My God!" exclaimed Stan. "How are we ever gonna get back to civilization?"

"Just follow Lloyd," said Mort. "He's never gone over a week yet without finding a cat house."

* * *

At Tony's engagement party, Tony and Alfredo were standing off in the corner.

"Know somethin'?" said Tony. "I slept with every girl here with the exception of my sister and my fiancée."

"That's real interestin'," remarked Alfredo. "Between the two of us, we've screwed them all!"

* * *

Two policemen carried Conrad, unconscious, into the hospital emergency room. "What happened?" asked the intern on duty.

"He was parked with this babe," said one of the cops, "and the girl claims that he suddenly began to fondle her breasts, and she became upset."

"And then what happened?"

"She lost control of herself and bit his penis."

*   *   *

She: You'd better go—my husband just drove up!

He: Where's the back door?

She: We don't have one.

He: Where would you like one?

*   *   *

CUNNING LINGUIST

*A lady well versed in the use
of her native tongue*

*   *   *

"I got a riddle for you, Rocky. What has one hundred and sixty-seven teeth and holds back a big monster?"

"Give up."

"My zipper!"

*   *   *

The baker beheld with affection
His upstanding pulsing erection.
    He said, "I am chaste,
    But it won't go to waste.
I'll poke doughnut holes to perfection."

*   *   *

* * *

Did you hear about the retired brassiere manufacturer who still liked to keep his hand in the business?

* * *

At an Atlanta cocktail party, the sweet southern gal was chatting with a New Yorker. "I declare, you'll never win an argument with me, because I'll give you tit for tat every time."

"Okay," he said. "Tat!"

* * *

Mary Lou came from Charleston. Her roommate Holly was born in the Bronx. One day, they were sitting in their living room discussing dudes.

"Boys in South Carolina work slow and easy when they want some," revealed Mary Lou. "First a boy holds your hand. Then he pats the top of your head. Then he kisses your cheek. Then he says you smell good. And then . . ."

"Hey!" interrupted Holly. "By that time, a New York stud has stripped, flipped, and zipped! And he's back in a phone booth trying to line up a date for the next night!"

* * *

Henderson entered a drugstore and asked the woman clerk for a male attendant. She assured him she would not be embarrassed, so he asked for condoms. "What size?"

"I don't know," said Henderson. "Do they come in sizes?"

"Come in the back here," she said, taking him behind the partition to the rear of the store. She spread her legs. "Put it in. All right. Size seven. Take it out. How many do you want?"

Henderson left the store in a daze and quickly told his friend Bolin all about it. Bolin immediately went to the store, pretended to be embarrassed, to want condoms and not to know his size. He was taken by the woman clerk into the back.

"Put it in. All right. Take it out. Size eight. How many do you want?"

Bolin waited and did not withdraw till he ejaculated. Then he said, "Oh, I don't want any right now. I just came in for a fitting."

Rita and Bob sat in a dark corner way up in an almost-deserted theater balcony. The couple embraced so passionately that Bob's toupee slid from his head. Groping to find it in the darkness, he reached under Rita's skirt.

"That's it, that's it," she moaned.

"It can't be," said Bob, "I part mine on the side."

*   *   *

Wally and his buddy Richie met in the company lunchroom during their coffee break. "I tell you, I'm really worried," whispered Wally. "I just got a letter from a guy threatening to kill me if I don't stop boffing his wife."

"So?" said Richie. "Why don't you just stay away from the broad?"

"But the guy didn't sign the letter!" said Wally.

*   *   *

Marilyn the receptionist was invited up to the sales manager's apartment to look at his etchings.

When they arrived at his flat, she was surprised to find no etchings at all. In fact, to her amazement, Marilyn discovered he had no chairs, no tables, no furniture.

She was floored.

DUDE DITTY

She was only a bookkeeper's daughter,
But she'd let anyone make an entry.

* * *

Felix was shacked up with Sheila, the girl he just picked up. In the middle of the night, he was awakened by screams. Felix woke up Sheila and asked, "What's that noise?"

"It sounds like the woman next door is having a fit!" she replied.

"Yeah," agreed Felix, "and a tight one at that."

* * *

A bunch of the boys up in Oregon were talking about the Long Dong Convention that took place in San Francisco.

"The guy who won had sixteen inches!"

"That's nothing," boasted Griswold, a lumberjack. "You call that big? Why once in Alaska I took out my pecker to pee, got to thinking of my girl, and couldn't get it back in my pants. It was so cold up there in Alaska I had to rub it with snow to keep it from freezing, and what I couldn't reach with my hands, I threw snowballs at."

* * *

As Cropton sat down in a Philadelphia bar, he noticed that each stool had a number painted on it. Sitting next to him was Lopez and a good-looking blonde. "Excuse me," asked Cropton, "do you know what these numbers mean?"

"Sure," answered the Mexican. "Every half hour, the bartender spins a wheel, and whoever has the winning seat gets to go upstairs for the wild sex orgy they have up there."

"That's terrific!" exclaimed Cropton. "Have you won?"

"Not yet," said Lopez, "but my date has—four times in a row."

* * *

There was a rich jockey named Knott
Who invited a girl to his yacht.
   Too lazy to rape her,
   He made darts of paper
Which he languidly threw at her twat.

* * *

"Stan really digs ballin', don't he?"
"You kiddin'? When Stan was a kid, he was so horny he was thrown out of the Boy Scouts for doing push-ups over gopher holes."

* * *

A tourist was told to go to a whore-house at 884 West 84th Street. By mistake, he went to 448 West 48th Street, which turned out to be a chiropodist's office. The out-of-towner figured the foot doctor's was just a front.

He walked in, and the nurse said to him, "Go behind that screen and get ready."

He took out his penis, and when the nurse came in to look, she exclaimed, "My God! That ain't a foot!"

"You gonna quibble about an inch?"

* * *

* * *

Did you hear about the guy who joined a nudist colony and on the first day stuck out like a sore thumb?

* * *

MACHO MELODY

She was only the elevator operator's daughter, but she would go down as well as up.

* * *

Turrell, an architect, Legett, an engineer, and Foster, a city planner, were enjoying a few brews at a local pub. During their chitchat the question Who created a woman? came up.

"It was an architect," proclaimed Turrell. "Look at the beauty of the lines."

"I think it was an engineer," said Legett. "It is a well-structured and proportioned body."

"I disagree," said Foster. "It had to be a city planner. Who else would put the playground so close to the waste disposal!"

* * *

There once was a girl named Sue Claire
Whose rump was all covered with hair.
When her beau dropped her draw-
ers,
He exclaimed with applause,
"You're lovely! You look like my
mare!"

* * *

Wheeler, who was highly sexed, had an erection at the slightest provocation when in the company of the opposite sex. He went to a doctor, who suggested that he simply tape the organ to his leg. Shortly after, the M.D. ran into Wheeler and asked whether his advice had worked.

"Everything went great 'til the end of my first date," reported Wheeler. "She had started up the steps of her house, and then she suddenly turned around and leaned down to kiss me. That's when I kicked her right in the face."

* * *

DUDE

A man who comes and then goes

* * *

Gianelli, a young newspaper reporter, was given the assignment of writing a feature story on a local nudist camp.

At the camp office, he obtained permission from Brimley, the owner. He was told that he couldn't wear clothing on the grounds and that he must behave himself at all times. Gianelli said that he understood. He went to the dressing room, took off his clothes, and began walking about.

Two hours later, Brimley found the reporter reclining on a chaise longue watching some girls taking an exercise class. His pecker pointed straight up like a flagpole.

"What in the hell did I tell you," screamed the owner. "No funny stuff is allowed in this place. Get your clothes and get out!"

"What are you talking about?" replied Gianelli.

"That's what I'm talking about," the owner said, pointing to the reporter's ramrod.

"Oh, that's just my sundial."

"Yeah. If that's a sundial, what time is it?"

The reporter studied himself a moment. "Eleven-fifteen."

"Ah ha! You liar! It's eleven-thirty!"

"I'll be damned. I forgot to wind it," Gianelli said as he began jacking off.

* * *

Senior Smiles

Iverson, a sixty-six-year-old stockbroker, was pouring his heart out to a friend.

"I'm nuts about this girl," he said. "Do you think I have a better chance of marrying her if I tell her I'm fifty?"

"I think you'll have a better chance if you tell her you're eighty."

* * *

Eighty-six-year-old Stebbens called on his physician.

"Doc, I'd like you to examine me, to see if I am sexually fit."

"Very well. Let me see your sex organs."

The aged patient replied, "Okay," and stuck out his index finger and his tongue.

* * *

A crafty old lecher named Matt
Loved to fondle the gals where they sat.
      If a girl weren't alert,
      He'd reach under her skirt
And claim to be petting a cat.

* * *

Tucker: Doc, I need a blood test. I'm gettin' married.

Doctor: Really? How old are you?

Tucker: I'll be eighty-eight next month.

Doctor: And how old is your bride-to-be?

Tucker: Just turned twenty-two.

Doctor: Do you realize that such a difference in ages could prove fatal?

Tucker: Well, if she dies, she dies!

* * *

How can you tell an old man in the dark?

It's not hard.

* * *

Bigelow sat reading the sports section when his wife walked in and said to him, "Don't you think I look younger without a bra?"

"You really do, dear," he answered. "It's drawn all the wrinkles out of your face."

Hadley was seventy and getting married for the sixth time. As he waited for the ceremony to begin, he thought of the songs that had been played at all his previous weddings.

When he married the first time, he was an athletic twenty. The band had played "There'll Be a Hot Time in the Old Town Tonight."

Hadley took his second wife at age thirty to the strains of "I'll Be Loving You, Always."

At forty, they played "Now and Then."

At fifty, he had danced to "Don't Get Around Much Any More."

His fifth wife had joined him when he was sixty. Their song was "The Thrill Is Gone."

Suddenly, his thoughts were interrupted by the church organ, announcing the beginning of the ceremony. He strode down the aisle as the organist played "Remember When."

* * *

Grandpa Parker was caught unprepared by the Michigan cold spell last winter and complained to his grandson that he hadn't been able to sleep.

"Did your teeth chatter, grandpa?"

"Dunno," he replied. "We didn't sleep together."

Betty Borden, the beautiful Brentwood homemaker, gets bravos with this bubbler:

The Kimberlys were about to celebrate their fiftieth wedding anniversary, and Mr. Kimberly promised his wife anything she wanted.

"Do you remember when you proposed to me?" she asked. "You got down on your knees and said, 'I love you.' That's what I'd like you to do again."

"Are you kiddin'?" He frowned.

"No, I'm serious."

"Okay," said Kimberly as he got down on both knees. "Dear, I love you. Now help me up!"

80

81

Fuller had reached the grand age of ninety-seven, but that wasn't the reason he phoned his son.

"Say," he announced, "my new young bride just presented me with a baby boy!"

Unable to believe his ears, the son pleaded, "Will you repeat that, please?"

"Hell, no," snapped the old man. "You darn fool, I didn't even do it the first time!"

* * *

A naughty old banker from Butte
Had a habit his friends thought was cute.
    He'd slip off to Ft. Wayne
    And then proceed from the train
To a house of distinct ill repute.

* * *

Old man Dudley was a steady client in a Pennsylvania house of horizontal refreshment.

One night, his favorite, Roxanne, was busy, and he refused to take anyone else.

"What's Roxanne got that the rest of my girls don't have?" asked the madam.

"Patience."

* * *

Blair, age seventy-three, went to a bordello and asked for a girl with gonorrhea.

The madam sent him upstairs to room 212. As the girl undressed, Blair asked if she had gonorrhea.

"Gonorrhea? I should say not!" she said.

The old man sent the girl downstairs, and the madam sent another girl, saying, "Crystal, you go up and tell him you got the clap. Okay?"

Crystal agreed and went upstairs. When Blair asked whether she had gonorrhea, the girl said, "Yeah!"

They got into bed together, and the union lasted about ten minutes. When it was over, the prostie said, "Listen, grandpa, I don't really have gonorrhea."

"Now you do," smiled the old man.

*   *   *

NEWS ITEM

Doctors say that people over sixty-five
still have their sex drive. It's
just that their clutch has a tendency
to slip.

*   *   *

Laura Manning, the lovely composer/musician, makes merry with this bit of mirth:

On a windy Chicago street corner, a still-attractive senior citizen held tightly to her hat with both hands while her skirt flew above her waist. Two men passing by noticed the gray-haired lady struggling with the elements. She smiled at them and huffed. "What you guys are looking at is sixty-eight years old. What I'm hanging on to is brand-new."

MacReedy, age ninety-three, strolled into the local bawdy house with a hunk of cotton in one hand and a condom in the other. "I want a nice young chick," said the old man.

"You must be joshin'," the madam said, sneering. "And what are you carrying that cotton and that rubber for?"

"Never mind. How much?"

"Okay, it's your funeral. Gimme a hundred. Go on up to room 109."

MacReedy went up to the room and knocked. The gal invited him in, and when she saw his snow-white hair, nearly fainted. "Hey, what you got that cotton and that condom for?"

"Put cotton in my nose and my ears. I hate to hear a woman scream, and I hate the smell of burning rubber!"

* * *

A traveling salesman stopped at a grocery store in a tiny Vermont town. As he bought some soda pop, he couldn't help noticing a couple of elderly men sitting close to the stove.

"Pop," he said, smiling, to one old codger, "can you remember the first girl you ever screwed?"

"Sonny," he remarked, "I can't even remember the last one."

Ninety-year-old Tomlin went to a cat house. He gave Linette, the hooker, a bang. Then another.

"The best ever!" cried the whore.

After the second time, Tomlin went to the bathroom and stayed in there for an hour. Linette became concerned and went in to see what happened. She found him playing with himself.

"What are you doin' that for?" she asked.

"I forgot," said the old man, "what I came here for!"

* * *

Octogenarians Akins and Stout were dating two charming old ladies at a summer resort. They decided to have a double wedding ceremony.

Immediately after, they went to their respective rooms and didn't meet again until the following morning. They began comparing notes.

"What a night I had with my bride," said Akins. "Three or four times. By the way, how did you do with yours?"

"Tell the truth," said his friend, "it slipped my mind completely."

* * *

* * *

Did you hear about the eighty-six-year-old man accused of rape who was acquitted because the evidence wouldn't stand up in court?

* * *

Slagel shuffled into the bawdy house, and the madam stared in amazement at his wrinkled face. "You gotta be in the wrong place," she exclaimed. "What're you lookin' for?"

"I want a girl" muttered the old man. "I wanna get laid."

"How old are you, pop?" asked the madam.

"Ninety-six."

"Ninety-six? Pop, you've *had* it!"

"Oh," said the old man, reaching for his wallet. "How much do I owe you?"

* * *

At a big midwestern university, the subject of sin came up in theology class.

The professor said, "Even a good man sins seven times a day. And at my age, at least six of those sins are bragging."

* * *

Collins went down to the social security office and was interviewed by a case worker. "Look," said the senior citizen, "I lost my card, but I really need the money. My wife is sick, and we don't have any food in the house."

"All right," said the interviewer, "open your shirt and let me see the hair on your chest."

Collins, a little surprised, did what the woman requested. "Okay," she said, "I believe you." The worker wrote a check for him.

Collins went home and explained exactly what happened, including the unorthodox method the woman used to determine his eligibility.

"What do you think of that?" he asked.

"Why didn't you drop your pants," said his wife, "you could've gotten total disability."

* * *

Old Panzinni walked briskly into a drugstore, strode over to the pharmacist, and said, "I would like a box of Sex-Lax."

"You mean Ex-Lax." The pharmacist smiled.

"No," said the Italian. "I don't have-a no trouble *going*."

* * *

Bob Todd, the super Sea Ranch real estate salesman, gets screams with this sidesplitter:

A well-shaped, extremely attractive silver-haired grandmother walked into a liquor store, pointed two guns at the proprietor, and said, "Give me six bottles of Scotch. And all the money. Then I want you to take me into the back room and give me a good screw."

He got the money and gave her the Scotch, then took her into the back room where he proceeded to make love to her with the guns still pointed at his head. In the excitement of the lovemaking, the woman dropped her guns.

"Please, lady," said the owner, "would you mind picking up your guns again—I'm expecting my wife any minute."

Old Professor Reynolds became engaged to one of his students and immediately went to the campus marital clinic for counseling.

The day before the wedding, Reynolds sat in the therapist's office.

"We're really interested in your case and would appreciate your telegraphing us a brief coded report as soon as possible," said the counselor. "If you feel generalized stirrings tomorrow night, word it 'Studying chemistry.' If you manage any sort of erection, make it 'Passed anthropology,' and if you score, by all means telegraph 'Received A in physics.'"

The oldster agreed.

Two mornings later, the message arrived. It read: FLUNKED EVERYTHING EXCEPT FRENCH.

*　　*　　*

Jaeger and Hanlon were long retired. Each Sunday afternoon found them passing time on a park bench. They watched couples strolling by, young lovers who were holding hands, kissing and hugging each other.

"What wouldn't I give," Jaeger sighed "to have just one more good, long screw!"

"In my case," retorted Hanlon, "I'd even settle for one more good, short premature ejaculation."

Yates and Watson, two old-timers, were relaxing in Central Park.

"My timing is terrible," stated Yates.

"What do you mean?" said Watson.

"Now that the sexual revolution has arrived, I seem to have run out of ammunition."

* * *

There was an old maid of Gibraltar
Who was raped as she knelt at the altar.
It really seems odd
That a virtuous God
Should answer her prayers and assault her.

* * *

Is an old maid's laughter "He! He! He!?"

* * *

Brenda visited her elderly spinster Aunt Aurelia. "How're you feelin'?" she asked.

"Okay," replied the old gal. "But, oh, how I long for the good old days when the postman always came twice."

* * *

*   *   *

Billings stayed in an old English bed-and-breakfast hotel with the bathroom down the hall. He didn't have a bathrobe and took a chance on running to the bathroom naked. Three old maids from Daytona got off the elevator as he was halfway down the hall. Billings froze and pretended to be a statue.

One old maid put a nickel in his mouth.

The second put a dime.

The third put in a quarter and shook his penis. "Look, girls," she cried, "hand lotion!"

*   *   *

Gretchen and Josephine were riding in their chauffeur-driven limousine when it hit a cow on a country road. The old girls were considerably shaken. When they came to, Gretchen saw a cow's teats in her lap.

"My God!" cried Gretchen, "the chauffeur's been killed!"

*   *   *

Did you hear about the old maid who got tired of using candles?

She called in an electrician.

*   *   *

Aunt Maisie was bothered by intense itching below the waistline and visited a doctor. He examined the area very closely and announced, "You have a case of crabs!"

"Impossible!" she sputtered. "I bathe at least three times a day. And change all my clothes each time. I've never even been with a man in my life. I still have my cherry!"

"Okay," replied the doctor, "I'll check again."

He went back into his lab. He returned in a few moments and announced, "Would you believe fruit flies?"

* * *

"I'm accustomed," said aging Miss Tudor,
To the burglar who'd finally screwed her.
   "To carrots and candles
   And john-plunger handles,
So you, sir, are just an intruder!"

* * *

SPINSTER

A do-it-yourself expert.

* * *

Aunt Agnes was given a surprise birthday party by her relations. As she prepared to cut her cake, a worldly young niece offered, "Now remember, auntie, you're supposed to make a wish *before* you blow out the candles!"

"I know," snapped the spinster, "but if I get my wish, I won't need the candles!"

*   *   *

What's the difference between a fat woman and an old maid?

The fat woman is trying to diet; the old maid is dying to try it.

*   *   *

Miss Prudence, a maiden lady, phoned a Baltimore police station in hysterics. Little children in the street beneath her window were chalking dirty words on the sidewalk. Desk Sergeant Crawford asked how old the kids were and what they were writing. Miss Prudence estimated their ages and insisted someone come by and correct them at once.

"Lady," said the officer, "they don't need correcting. It is just a stage of being naughty that all kids go through."

"Well," she barked, "they certainly do need correcting. They're spelling prick with a capital P and pussy with only one 's'!"

HERE LIES ANN MANN.
SHE LIVED AN OLD MAID
AND DIE AN OLD MANN.

Bridget and Augusta, two elderly matrons, were riding the Thursday afternoon train back to the suburbs. "What did you do in Boston?" asked Augusta.

"I went to get scrod."

"So did I, dear," whispered Bridget, "but I didn't know that was the past tense."

* * *

Did you hear about the old maid who uses a pickle for self-satisfaction?

Her birth control dill.

* * *

Kendall and Jordan, two young California surfers, were beautifully tanned except for their genital areas. Kendall came up with an idea. "Let's go down to the end of the beach tomorrow and bury ourselves in the sand with just our joy sticks exposed."

"You got it," agreed Jordan. "A couple of sessions like that and our tans ought to even out nicely."

Next morning, the boys did just that. In a few minutes, two vacationing spinster schoolteachers happened on the unusual sight.

"Oh, look, Letitia!" exclaimed one. "I would have done anything to get one of those when I was younger—and now, my God, they're growing wild!"

98

* * *

MOTH

*The only thing that ever gets
into a spinster's pants in a dark place*

* * *

Said an old maid one fondly remembers,
  "Now my days are quite clearly Sep-
tembers.
      All my fires have burned low,
      I'll admit that it's so,
But you still might have fun in the
embers."

* * *

Miss Marcella was clerking at a neigh-
borhood dime store. Another old maid came
in and asked, "Do you have foot-long
candlesticks?"

"Say," barked Miss Marcella, "can't
you think of anything *decent* to talk about?"

* * *

Girls who scream and girls who tell
    Will grow up spinsters sure as hell.

* * *

Millicent and Polly, two maiden ladies, were conducting a school survey. They went to a suburban house and knocked on the door. It was answered by a man who had been taking a shower and was covering himself with only a newspaper. He told them, "I'm Peter Pepperpod; wife Pauline; sons Paul and Peter, Jr., both in school. I am a peanut packer for Planter's Peanuts and poke around in part-time party planning on the side."

Later, Millicent went to the ladies room at an Arco filling station and did not come out for twenty minutes. "What happened?" asked Polly.

"I just sat there and got to thinking about that personable Mr. Peter Pepperpod, the peanut packer for Planter's Peanuts and part-time party planner, standing there with his pert, petrified pivot poking through the paper, and it just made my pussy pucker with such peccability that I couldn't hardly precipitate!"

* * *

MISSISSIPPI MELODY

She was just a country old maid—always waiting at the gate but never gettin' any mail in her box.

* * *

Olive, a love-starved spinster, was so desperate that she went to a newspaper office to place an ad under "Situations Wanted." When she asked the young clerk the rates, he said, "We charge a minimum of five dollars for each insertion."

"You don't say?!" Olive retorted. "Then here's twenty dollars, and to hell with the ad!"

Marital Merries

Thatcher was going over his wife's latest bills from Bloomingdale's.

"Why do you have to buy such expensive bras?" he snapped. "You certainly don't have much to put in them."

"If that's the way you figure," she replied, "then you haven't needed a new pair of shorts in years!"

* * *

Pritchard returned from a convention and proudly showed his wife a case of Chivas Regal he'd won for having the largest sex organ of all present. "What!" she exclaimed. "You mean to tell me you exhibited yourself in front of all those people?"

"Aah, honey," he replied, "only enough to win."

* * *

* * *

Said an ardent young bridegroom named Trask,
"I will grant any wish that you ask."
        Said his bride, "Screw me, dearie,
        Until I grow weary,"
But he died of old age at the task.

* * *

What did the banker's wife say to her husband on their wedding night?

"Don't forget, there's a penalty for early withdrawal."

* * *

VAGINAL JELLY

The hole schmear

* * *

Wayland: I never had any relations with my wife before we were married. Did you?

Viviani: I don't know. What was her maiden name?

* * *

* * *

Mrs. Nagel approached her husband one morning and said, "Honey, I've got good news and bad news. The good news is I think it's time for a second honeymoon."

"What's the bad news?" asked Mr. Nagel.

"I'd like to take it with a second husband."

* * *

McVee sat in Dr. Dixon's office after his examination.

"How often do you have intercourse with your wife?" asked the physician.

"Three times a day!" replied the patient.

"And, ah, I suppose, also, with your secretary?"

"Three times a day."

"I see," said the M.D. "And the maid, too, no doubt?"

"Three times a day."

"Any other women?" The doctor sneered.

"Three times a day."

"Good Lord! You're killing yourself. Why don't you take yourself in hand?"

"Three times a day!"

* * *

Bernie Wayne, one of America's great songwriters, breaks up buddies with this bon mot:

After working late one evening, Lacy stopped to have a drink at a cocktail lounge and struck up a conversation with Kroll at the bar.

"One thing I've learned in my long experience with the fair sex," said Kroll, "is that you can't trust a woman with brown eyes!"

"Wow!" exclaimed Lacy. "I've been married two years, and I just realized I don't know what color eyes my wife has."

He bolted from the bar and headed home. His wife was in bed asleep. Creeping closer Lacy lifted her eyelid. "Brown, my God!" he roared.

A man crawled out from under the bed and said, "How the devil did you know I was here?"

107

A handsome young gasman from Chester
Surprised a blonde housewife called Hester.
> Said he, "This is sweeter
> Than reading your meter,"
So they then took a lengthy siesta.

* * *

Logan returned from a four-week business trip and lay down beside his wife, who was dreaming she was making love to her boyfriend. Soon he was asleep.

Suddenly, in her dream, Mrs. Logan imagined she heard a familiar step outside the bedroom door.

"Oh, my God!" she cried aloud in her sleep. "Get out, my husband's coming!"

So Logan leaped out of bed and ran into the closet.

* * *

Blanchard arrived home unexpectedly and found his wife lying in bed. He stared suspiciously at a cigar smouldering in the ash tray beside the bed.

"Where did that cigar come from?" he bellowed.

The bathroom door opened and a shaky masculine voice said, "Cuba!"

* * *

Why are electric trains like a woman's boobs?

Because they are originally intended for children, but it's the fathers who play with them.

* * *

Denker discovered his wife in bed with another man.

"What's the meaning of this?" he demanded. "Who is this guy?"

"That seems like a fair question," said the wife, rolling over. "What's your name, fella?"

* * *

Did you hear about the recently divorced choir singer who chased her boy friend all over the church and finally caught him by the organ?

* * *

MATE SWAPPING

Intermarital extracourse

* * *

To my loving wife:

During the past year I have tried to seduce you 365 times. I have succeeded a total of 26 times. This averages once every two weeks. The following is a list of reasons for my failure:

Not in the mood.	15
Headache.	18
Too drunk.	7
Giggles.	4
Wrong time of month.	12
Window open, neighbors will hear.	9
Backaches.	16
Too full.	2
Company in guest room.	13
Grease on face.	2
Watching The Late Show.	17
Watching The Early Show.	7
Kids are crying.	21
Mud pack.	5
Reading the paper.	2
Have to go potty.	19
We will wake the children.	16
Foot aches.	2
Pretending to be asleep.	49
It's too hot.	5
It's too cold.	5
It's too late.	18
It's too early.	23
Too tired.	52
Total	339

Do you think you can improve your record this year?

P.S. Out of the 26 successful times:

12 times you said hurry up and get it over with.

3 times you chewed gum all the time.

4 times you watched TV all the time.

6 times I had to wake you and tell you we were done.

And, one time I thought I had hurt you—because I felt you move.

Signed _____

* * *

The morning after his wedding, Jameson, a Madison Avenue advertising exec, sat brooding over a drink in his favorite bar.

"What's the trouble?" asked the bartender. "You should be the happiest guy in the world today."

"What creatures of habit we are," he said. "This morning, when I arose, half asleep, without thinking, I pulled a fifty-dollar bill from my wallet and left it on the pillow."

"That's nothin,' " said the barkeep. "Your wife won't think anything of it."

"You don't understand," he said. "Half asleep, without thinking, she gave me twenty dollars change."

* * *

*   *   *

In summer, he said she was fair;
In autumn, her charms were still there.
     But he said to his wife
     In the winter of life,
  "There's no spring in your old der-
riere."

*   *   *

Why is it a witch never has a baby?
Because her husband has a Halloweeny!

*   *   *

Rip and Jess were having a few drinks
at a swinging bar. "Wow, look at the pair
of boobs that just bounced in!" announced
Rip. "I wonder if she'd let me have a little."
    "If she does, let me know," said Rip.
"I'm her husband!"

*   *   *

Denny: What's the matter? You look
         worried.
Styles: I'm gonna be a father.
Denny: What's so awful about that?
Styles: Nothing—except my wife doesn't
         know it yet!

*   *   *

Bessie Mae wanted a divorce because of her husband's inordinate sexual demands.

"Have you filed your affidavit?" said her lawyer.

"Filed it? It's so sore I can't even touch it!"

* * *

A horse-loving lady named Maud
At love was a terrible fraud;
    With the boys in the stable,
    She was willing and able,
But in bed with her spouse she was bored.

* * *

Peggy's marriage ceremony came off perfectly, but as a wedding-night prank, her little sister had sewed the legs of Peggy's pajamas closed. The bride became hysterical when her foot would not go through.

"I can't get it in," she cried excitedly to her new husband. "You'll have to cut it open a little with your pocket knife."

From behind the door, Peggy's mother screamed, "Don't cut it! Don't cut it! It'll stretch. Mine did!"

* * *

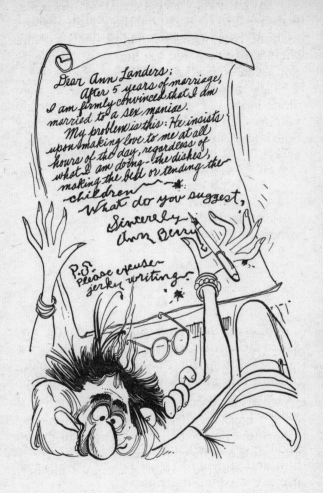

Dear Ann Landers:
After 5 years of marriage,
I am firmly convinced that I am
married to a sex maniac.
My problem is this: He insists
upon making love to me at all
hours of the day, regardless of
what I am doing — the dishes,
making the bed or tending the
children —.
What do you suggest,
Sincerely
Ann Berry

P.S.
Please excuse
jerky writing.

At a wedding reception, Bitsy, the bride, and her girl friends overheard the groom making bets with his buddies. "I'm sure she's a virgin," said her husband. "I'll give you odds of five to one!"

Later, when the two honeymooners were alone in the car, she screeched, "How could you *do* such a thing? We're only married an hour, and already you're throwing money away!"

* * *

Horace snuggled up to his wife and asked for a little loving.

"Darling, don't be like that," she said. "Don't talk about loving when the children can hear. If you're interested, just ask me if you can use my washing machine."

The next night, she was the one who had the urge, and she snuggled over close to him and sighed, "Dear, would you like to use my washing machine?"

"No, love bug," he replied. "I only had a small bundle tonight, so I used the hand laundry!"

Wife:	You're taking an awfully long time tonight!
Husband:	I just can't think of anybody!

The phone rang, and Angelo picked it up. "Hey, Angelo, it's Sal. I got two passes to the hockey game tonight. You wanna go?"

"Thanks," said Angelo, "but I can't. Novak's playin' tonight."

The following evening, Salvatore called again. "Got passes to a Knicks game for tonight. You interested?"

"Can't make it," said Angelo. "Novak's playin' tonight."

The next night, Sal tried again. "Got two good seats for the fights tonight. How about it?"

"Sorry. Novak's playin' tonight," said Angelo.

"Wait a second," said Salvatore. "What does this guy Novak play?"

"I don't know," replied Angelo. "I never even met him. I don't know what he plays, and I don't know where he plays, but when Novak's playin', I'm screwin' around with his wife."

TRIAL MARRIAGE

Riding the horse before you buy it

* * *

Irate housewife: My husband can lick your husband.

Second housewife: I think he does.

* * *

Do you guys wanna know what women go through in childbirth?

Pull your lips over your head!

* * *

Dorothy and Jeff were drinking heavily at a night club when Jeff slid under the table. A fellow nearby said to Dorothy, "Lady, your husband just slid under the table!"

"No," she replied. "He couldn't have. My husband just walked in!"

* * *

Doctor: What makes you think your wife is frigid?

Parrish: Well, last night when she opened her mouth to say "No!" a little light came on!

Gizella Wildman, the gorgeous Hungarian glass queen, gets guffaws with this gut grabber:

Louis the lion tamer was a very courageous man. Even the most vicious lion did not frighten him. He feared no king of the jungle. However, he was afraid of the woman he married. She did not like him to stay out late. One night, Louis had a few drinks with the circus performers, and when he realized the lateness of the hour, he was too frightened to confront his wife. Scared to death of going home, Louis crawled into the lion's cage and went to sleep with his head resting on the largest lion.

Early the next morning, his wife began to look for him. She searched all over town before she came to the menagerie where he worked. There she discovered him in the lion's cage. She glared at him and then shouted with contempt, "You coward!"

118

	I have a headache!	My back hurts!
You just want me for my body!	What do you mean, what am I saving it for? Don't talk dirty!	You want me to what? You pervert!
I'd love to, dear, but it's that time again!	Ditto	Ditto
Ditto	I forgot to take the pill.	I'm too sleepy.
What are you trying to do, rape me?	It's three o'clock in the morning! Are you out of your mind?	No! And don't give me that "honeymoon is over" jazz!

* * *

There was a young Latin named Manny
The size of whose dong was uncanny.
His wife, the poor dear,
Took it into her ear,
And it came out the hole in her fanny.

Calendar

Is that all you ever think about?	I'm not mentally in the mood.	I want to watch the Late Late Show.	All right! All right! But hurry up; it's ten-thirty already!
It's too early.	It's too late.	Before dinner?	All right, you sex fiend.
Ditto	Ditto	Ditto	Ditto
Honey, not tonight. I'm out of pills!	In broad daylight? You beast!	It might as well be no!	Didn't I tell you? I'm staying at mother's tonight.
With the lights on? What do you think I am?			

* * *

Husband: You said there was a burglar in the house while I was away? Did he get anything?

Wife: I'll say he did. I thought it was you.

Dr. Hotchkiss, the plastic surgeon, prepared to do a testicle implant. He was assisted by Baxter, a new young intern. The surgeon advised the intern to carve up a silicone implant for him while he prepared the patient's scrotum.

The eager Baxter, however, dropped the implant just as he finished preparing it, and it shattered into a million pieces on the floor. When Dr. Hotchkiss called for the implant in the operating room next door, the young man panicked. He grabbed a scallion from his lunch bag, cut off the green stalk, and carried it in. The onion was sewn into the scrotum and the patient sent home.

A month later, Baxter nervously undressed the onion-implanted scrotum and tried not to look nervous as he asked the patient, "Well, how are you doing?"

"Not bad, doc," answered the patient. "I've noticed only three things! When I urinate, I get a burning sensation, when I make love to my wife, she gets heartburn, and when I drive past a MacDonald's, I get an erection."

* * *

MONOGAMIST

A man with a one-crack mind.

Carlson the mortician was laying out the body of a man with an extremely long penis. He called in Eunice, the receptionist, and showed it to her. "That's just like my husband's," said the woman.

"What?" exclaimed the funeral director. "You mean to say he's got one that long?"

"Well, not exactly! But it's just as dead!"

* * *

Panatelli was perusing *The Joy of Sex,* and his wife asked why.

"I'm tired of being in the same old rut," he replied.

"But I don't understand," she protested.

"Well," said the Italian, "let me put it to you another way."

* * *

Dr. Mason had just completed his examination. "Mr. Jardine," he said, "I've got some very bad news for you!"

"What is it?" asked the man.

"You've got cancer of the penis!"

Jardine rushed home, grabbed his wife, and began cuffing her around. "I've got cancer of the prick," he shouted. "I told you to stop smoking!"

123

Kid Kidding

Little Donald was bragging about his father's bravery to a schoolmate.

"He's a volunteer fireman. He goes out during the night, while that coward Mr. Walton next door comes over without even waiting to dress, gets into bed with mama, and was so scared that the bed shook something terrible."

* * *

Mrs. Nelson was saying good night to her children. In order to prepare them for the birth of her next child, she told them that the stork brings babies.

After she kissed them and left, the little boy turned to his sister and remarked, "I don't care what mom says. I can't picture dad having sex with a stork."

* * *

Little Roy: I found a contraceptive on the veranda.
Little Ned: What's a veranda?

* * *

"Mama?"
"Yes, darling!"
"I know why daddy has such a big belly. I saw the baby sitter blowing it up last night."

* * *

While out driving in the country, little Lizabeth saw her father urinating. "How many of those have you got, daddy?"
"Only one, why?"
"Well, what did you do with the great big one you stuck in mama this morning?"

* * *

The elevator of a New Orleans sky-scraper was jam packed. Suddenly, a tall man screamed in sheer agony. Then a small boy said, "I don't care, mama! It was in my face, so I bit it!"

* * *

The bridge club ladies had assembled at the McAllister home and were busily chatting while playing their trumps. Suddenly, six-year-old Parnell burst into the room brandishing a large kitchen knife. The youngster was chasing the family cat, and as he ran through the room, he shouted: "When I catch you, I'll skin you alive, you little sonuvabitch."

Mrs. McAllister smiled politely. "And he can do it, too," she said. "He's such a husky little bastard."

* * *

Maynard sat down beside his mother and said, "Mommy, is it true that people can be taken apart like machines?"

"Of course not," replied his mother. "Where did you hear such nonsense?"

"Well, just now, daddy was talking to somebody on the phone, and I heard him say that last night he screwed the ass off his secretary."

Whitney woke up in the middle of the night and began crying. His mother came in and asked what the problem was. "I have to make a pee pee!" said the child.

"All right," said his mother. "I'll take you to the bathroom."

"No," wailed the youngster, "I want grandma."

"Don't be silly. I can do the same thing as grandma."

"No. Her hands shake."

* * *

Cameron was caught by his mother playing with himself. "You keep doing that," she warned, "and you'll go blind!"

"Can't I just do it until I need glasses?"

* * *

Reynolds sat his son down for some friendly fatherly advice.

"My boy, while it is no longer considered true that constant masturbating will lead to insanity or blindness—a quaint delusion of the Victorian age—I think you should know that according to the latest medical opinion, it can be the cause of a serious reduction in hearing."

"What?" said the boy.

* * *

The Dawsons stood outside the bedroom door listening to Styles say his prayers: "God bless daddy, God bless mommy, God bless sister Becky, and God bless grandma."

"Wonder why he didn't include grandpa in his prayers?" asked Mrs. Dawson.

The next day, they received a telegram that grandpa had died of a heart attack. That night, the Dawsons listened once again outside Styles's bedroom. "God bless daddy, God bless mommy, and God bless sister Becky."

"He left out grandma this time," said Dawson.

The next day, grandma fell down a flight of stairs and died of a broken neck. That evening, they listened outside the boy's bedroom, "God bless mommy and God bless sister Becky."

"He left me out," whispered Dawson.

"Just be extra careful tomorrow," advised his wife.

The next day, Dawson came home somewhat relieved that nothing had befallen him. "Anything unusual happen today?" he asked.

"No," said his wife, "but the milkman died."

* * *

It was close to midnight in a suburban area when a patrol car noticed a little boy walking along the street. He had his belongings in a bundle over his shoulder and was obviously running away. The police officer asked him, "Where are you goin'?"

"Last night, as I passed my parents' bedroom, papa was hollering, 'Here I go!' and mama was screaming, 'Wait for me!' and I figured why should I get stuck with an eighty-thousand-dollar mortgage?"

131

* * *

INCEST

*A dandy game the whole family
can play*

* * *

"You don't seem to like the new house-keeper," said Mrs. Stebbens to her young son.

"I hate her," screamed the kid. "I'd like to grab her and bite her on the back of the neck like daddy does."

* * *

When Tully left for work, his four-year-old son Tommy went to his mother. "When you're not home, mommy," said the boy, "daddy takes the maid upstairs and—"

"Hold it!" she interrupted. "Tell me the rest tonight when your father gets home."

At dinner that night, she said, "All right, Tommy, you may finish your story."

"Well, last Sunday, when you weren't home," said Tommy, "daddy took the maid upstairs and did to her what you and Uncle George do when daddy's gone fishing!"

* * *

Mrs. Peck sat in the child psychologist's office listening to his advice.

"I can assure you that there's nothing to be concerned about," said the shrink. "Masturbation in the case of a boy your son's age is quite normal."

"Perhaps," declared the woman, "but not in church!"

* * *

Rutledge was quite concerned because his ten-year-old, Nicholas, had a breast fixation. Whenever they'd pass a woman on the street or in a store, the boy would poke his father and exclaim, "Hey, Dad, did you see the tits on that one?"

After many embarrassing encounters, Rutledge got the kid into psychotherapy. Finally, after six months, the shrink pronounced the boy cured.

Rutledge took Nicholas out for a test walk. They passed several well-endowed women, and the kid didn't bat an eye. Elated, they caught the bus home. They boarded the bus, and as they were walking down the aisle to get their seats, the boy tapped his father and said, "Hey, dad, did you catch the ass on that bus driver?"

* * *

Alfred was walking with his father when they came upon two dogs in the mating position. "What are they doing, daddy?" asked the boy.

"They're making a puppy," replied his father.

That night, on his way to the bathroom, Alfred passed his parents' bedroom and saw them making love. "What are you doing, daddy?" asked the child.

"Mother and I are making you a baby brother."

"Yeah?" said Alfred. "Well, flip her over. I'd much rather have a puppy."

* * *

One morning during class, ten-year-old Justine asked the teacher, "Can a twenty-one-year-old girl have a baby?"

"Yes," replied the teacher.

"Can a seventeen-year-old girl have a baby?" persisted the girl.

"Yes!"

"Can a ten-year-old girl have a baby?"

"No. I'm afraid not," the teacher replied.

Just then, a boy sitting back of Justine tapped her on the shoulder and said, "You see, I told you you had nothin' to worry about!"

* * *

* * *

Talbert came home from school and announced to his mother, "I ain't gonna wear my V-neck sweater no more."

"Why not?" asked his mother.

"Teacher had on a sweater just like it, and when she bent over, one of her lungs fell out!"

* * *

One evening, up in their room, Delvin asked his big brother Bob, "When you get a hard-on, where does all the extra skin and meat come from?"

"Think it must come from the brain," replied Bob, "because when I get horny, I just don't have any sense at all!"

* * *

Norbert had been spending a great deal of his time in the bathroom. His worried parents took him to a doctor, who declared, "Your son is highly addicted to overproduction of orgasms through manual manipulation of the genital organs."

"Wow!" exclaimed the father, "and all this time I thought he was just beating his meat too much."

* * *

135

Willard:	Please, teacher, Eugenia has just wet her pants.
Teacher:	You shouldn't say that. You should put your hand up.
Willard:	I did. That's how I know.

* * *

"Our principal's main job is to keep all the mothers happy."

"How does he do that?"

"I don't know. He always shuts his office when they go in there."

* * *

"Children," instructed Miss Petty, "every morning, you should all take a cold shower. It will make you feel rosy all over. And now are there any questions?"

"Yes, teacher," said Stanley. "Tell us more about Rosie."

* * *

Teacher:	Can anyone in this class spell "Peter"?
Lee:	P-E . . . Oh, that's too hard for me.
Rory:	P-E-T . . . Gosh, that's too long for me.
Ava:	P-E-T-E-R. They don't come too long or too hard for me.

136

Miss Trent asked fifth graders the question "Who made you?"

Paul replied, "God!"

Walter answered, "The angels!"

Irene said, "You mean lately?"

* * *

NIGHTTIME VOICES

"Daddy, if you'll get me a drink of water, I'll shake the bed for mama."

* * *

Loretta entered the greeting-card shop. "Can I help you, miss?" asked the clerk.

"Well—er—yes," replied the girl. "Do you have any Father's Day cards that say, 'To whom it may concern'?"

* * *

Barbara was being bathed with her baby brother. She pointed to his penis and began to cry. "I want one of those!"

"If you're a good little girl," said her mother, "you'll get one later."

"Yes," said her father, "and if you're a bad little girl, you'll get lots of them."

* * *

Little Lyle and his neighbor-playmate Aimee were making mud pies in the back yard. In a little while, they got around to an interesting game called "Undress." After they got ready to play, Aimee pointed at Lyle and asked, "What's that?"

"I don't know," replied the boy.

"Can I touch it?"

"Heck no!" he said. "You've torn yours off already!"

A little baby snake came home with tears in his eyes. The mommy snake said, "Why are you crying?"

The baby snake said, "It's the snakes next door. They won't let me hiss in their pit."

The mommy snake said, "Never mind that bunch. I knew them when they didn't have a pit to hiss in."

* * *

A squeamish teenager named Brand
Thought caressing his penis was grand.
　　But he viewed with distaste
　　The gelatinous paste
That it left in the palm of his hand.

* * *

The pretty cheerleader Felicity and her date Miles were in his parked car back of the athletic field. After thirty minutes of passionate petting, the teenage temptress whispered in his ear, "If I let you put it in, would it touch bottom?"

"No, it wouldn't," panted the boy. "They say in sex education that that's impossible."

"Good," whispered the girl. "I promised mama I wouldn't let you go all the way."

* * *

Mother:	Now that junior is sixteen, I think it's about time you had a chat with him about the facts of life. Tell him about the birds and the bees.
Father:	Okay, I'll have a talk with him. *(That evening, he called junior into the living room.)* Son, now that you're sixteen, your mother feels that we should have a talk about the facts of life. Remember last year we went to Atlantic City on vacation.
Son:	Yes, dad.
Father:	Remember those two girls we met on the beach.
Son:	Yes, dad.
Father:	And remember that night we took them back to their hotel?
Son:	Yes, dad.
Father:	And remember what happened after that?
Son:	Yes, dad.
Father:	Well, it's the same with the birds and the bees.

* * *

"My dear, you've been kissing young Fred,"
A much worried mother once said.
"Since six; it's now ten;
Do it just once again
And then think of going to bed."

One evening in Los Angeles, Van Dyke was sitting in the living room reading the *Herald Examiner* when his fifteen-year-old daughter said, "Dad, can I ask you something which will affect my life from now on?"

"Of course, dear," he replied. "What is it?"

She said, "What's vice?"

Van Dyke dropped his newspaper and stammered, "S-s-sit down, honey, and I'll tell you."

He went through the Ten Commandments, paying particular attention to the subject of adultery. After two hours of graphic description, he sat back and said, "Now you know about vice. Why did you decide to ask me today?"

"Well," said the daughter, "today I made vice captain of the basketball team, and I wondered what it meant."

* * *

Maurine admitted to her mother that she'd fooled around on a date but that Dominic just maybe got in about a half an inch.

Each night following, further progress was reported until Maurine finally revealed that he had "put in about, er, nine inches."

"You be careful," shouted her mother, "or that man'll rape you!"

142

* * *

One night, Nelson decided to phone his eighteen-year-old daughter at her dormitory. He just wanted to remind her that the next day was her mother's birthday. When a man answered the call, Nelson almost had a heart attack.

"Don't be so upset," counseled the male voice. "We've been meaning to tell you. Your daughter and I are engaged."

"In what?" roared the father.

* * *

Father: Why does that fellow take you out on dates?

Daughter: Because he wants to.

Father: Wants to what?

* * *

Mr. Gaffey, the high school hygiene teacher, was lecturing on social diseases. "People claim they contacted veedee from toilets or drinking glasses," said Gaffey, "but how is the only proven way to get infected?"

The school's star quarterback bellowed from the rear: "From intersections!"

"Wait a minute." The teacher laughed. "You mean from 'intercourse,' don't you?"

"No, intersections," said the teenager. "I've caught it twice, and both times I picked up the chicks on street corners."

143

Carlyle, not wishing to impose his generation's views on today's youth, was unusually patient with his teenage daughter. However, his patience was almost exhausted one night as he watched the girl hold the telephone for fifteen minutes without saying a word.

Finally, he broke into the "conversation" and demanded to know why she had called her girl friend and not spoken one word.

"Oh," came the reply, "she told me to hold on until she finished laying her boy friend!"

Russell and York were talking about the up-coming generation.

"These teenagers nowadays, with their skin-tight pants, fancy hairdos, and high-heeled shoes, are really something," complained Russell.

"Yeah," agreed York, "and the girls are even worse."

* * *

Chris, aged fifteen, told his mother, "I just got laid today." His mother sent him directly to his room.

When his father got home that evening, he told him, "Son, women don't understand things like that, but I do. I was young once myself. How did you like it?"

"Great, dad. I can hardly wait till the next time!"

"Fine. When do you expect that to be?"

"I don't know for sure. As soon as my ass isn't sore anymore."

* * *

Thaddeus just got out of high school and went to work at a factory. One morning, he told his father, "Pop, I am now a man. I got my first blow job last night at the factory."

"How do you like it, son?"

"Terrible!" said the boy. "The taste in my mouth is awful."

146

Little Bobby walked into his parents' bedroom while they were making love. "What're you doing?" asked the child.

"Why, er, we're playing poker, son," replied his father.

"What's mama doing?"

"She's my partner."

Bobby ambled out of the bedroom, and as he walked down the hall, he heard noises in his sister's bedroom. He opened the door and discovered the girl having intercourse with her boy friend. "What're you doing?" asked Bobby.

"We're playing poker," replied his sister.

"And what about him?" asked the child, pointing to her sister's pal.

"He's my partner."

The youngster left and went down the hall to the room of Roger, his teenage brother, who was masturbating furiously. "What're you doing?" asked the child.

"I'm playing poker," replied Roger.

"Where's your partner?"

"Listen," said the older brother, "when you've got a good hand, you don't need a partner!"

* * *

Sally loved music with a passion. She needed to have every new record that came out. One summer, she sat on the beach listening to her radio when she heard a fellow singing "Two Lips and Seven Kisses." "I've got to get that record," she exclaimed.

Sally rushed to the phone to call a record store but by mistake dialed Arthur's Auto Body. "Hello," jawed Arthur.

"Have you got 'Two Lips and Seven Kisses?' asked the excited teenager.

"No," said the mechanic. "I got two balls and six inches."

"Is that a new record?"

"No, it's about average!"

* * *

GI Giggles

An army doctor was examining a new enlisted man at Fort Dix. When the young man had stripped naked, he said, "You don't seem to have much there."

"Just wink at it, doc," said the boy, "and see what happens."

* * *

Private First Class Jensen was on a twenty-four-hour pass and went to a dance in town. He met a very pretty waitress, and as they danced, he romanced her. Finally, he gasped. "Look, honey, I really dig you in a big way. But I don't have much time. I gotta be back in the morning. I'd sure like to speed things up between us."

"Well," said the gal, "I'm dancing as fast as I can!"

* * *

*   *   *

Private Hawkins served a two-year hitch in Europe and nearly flipped his lid over the French mademoiselles. He spent every thirty-six-hour pass and all of his furlough in Paris. Now that he was discharged, he returned to his Arkansas farm and the girl he left behind.

The first night home, he took his sweetheart out for a ride. He parked the car on a lonely road and began caressing her.

"Shall I pull up my dress?" she asked timidly.

"Not yet. First spit out that chewing gum!"

*   *   *

"Tell me, colonel," said the camp doctor, "when did you last have sex?"

"Er, let me see. Yes, 1945."

"That's a long time ago, 1945?"

"I dunno. It's only 2000 hours now."

*   *   *

The spouse of a pretty young thing
Came home from the wars in the spring.
    He was lame, but he came
    With his hand on his cane.
A discharge is a wonderful thing.

*   *   *

150

A big tough WAC sergeant ordered all of the cute new recruits to take one step forward. After a half dozen or so stepped out, she continued. "Now the rest of you swingers keep your mitts off these broads—they're mine!"

* * *

After finishing basic training, Zimbriski was shipped out and wrote home, "Dear parents, I'm not allowed to tell you where I am, but yesterday I shot big polar bear."

A few months later, he wrote, "Dear parents, our outfit was transferred, and I still can't tell you where I am, but last night I danced with hula girl."

A couple of weeks later, he wrote again, "Dear parents, I still can't tell you where I am, but today doctor told me I should have danced with polar bear and shot hula girl."

* * *

Johnson noticed Simpkins wearing a chest full of medals. "Hey, baby," asked Johnson, "whatcha get all those medals for?"

"Gunnery," replied the other black man.

"Gonerrhe? How you like that! I done had it for years, and they never even gave me a furlough!"

During army camouflage training, Private Yarnell, disguised as a tree trunk, made a sudden move that was spotted by a general.

"You idiot!" bellowed the officer. "You're supposed to be a tree. Don't you realize that by jumping and yelling the way you did, you could have endangered the lives of the entire company?"

"Yes, sir," said Yarnell. "But if I may say so, I did stand still when a flock of pigeons used me for target practice. I never moved a muscle when three bloodhounds thought I was a latrine. But when two squirrels ran up my pants leg and I heard the bigger one say, 'Let's eat one now and save the other until winter!' that did it!"

Private First Class Dinelli had a two-day pass. As he stepped off the train, his girl friend Gilda met him and threw her arms around him.

They were walking down the platform, chatting amiably, when all of a sudden they broke into a loud argument. The shouting between them became so intense that soon a crowd formed.

Finally, another soldier, waiting for a train, inquired, "Say, buddy, what's going on? What's the matter?"

Instead of answering, Dinelli kept shouting to his girl, "F.F.," while Gilda kept shouting back, "E.F."

"What's E.F.?" asked the soldier.

Dinelli replied, "She wants to eat first."

*   *   *

Eula Mae was visiting a soldier in the hospital.

"Where was you wounded?" the black girl asked.

"In the Philippines," he answered.

"Dat's terrible!" she exclaimed. "Is they any better now?"

*   *   *

Did you hear about the whore who liked the soldiers at Fort Bragg but had trouble taking care of all of them?

She put a wig on her fanny and opened up a second front!

Did you hear about the PX waitress who warned two Polish corporals that she had syphilis?

They didn't know what the word meant, so they looked it up in the dictionary, found it was a "disease of the privates," and being corporals, screwed her, anyway.

* * *

Ten thousand GIs from Fort Knox
Lined up in Kentucky for blocks
    For a chance to meet Millie;
    Half the gang banged her silly,
And the rest shot their wad in their socks.

* * *

Corporal Lawton received a two-week furlough so he could marry his childhood sweetheart. As the honeymoon neared its ending, Lawton telegraphed his commanding officer:

IT IS WONDERFUL HERE. REQUEST ONE WEEK'S EXTENSION OF FURLOUGH.

The reply:

IT IS WONDERFUL ANYWHERE. RETURN TO CAMP AT ONCE.

* * *

During the period of the Vietnam war, Carmack the draft evader crossed the Canadian border and hid out in a nunnery. After it got dark, he whispered to one of the nuns, "You know, sister, you've got two of the prettiest legs I've ever seen."

"Yes?" said the nun. "Well, get your hand out of there, because I've got two of the prettiest balls you ever saw, also. I don't want to go to Vietnam, either!"

A GI came home on furlough and made love to his wife Angelina so violently she sued for a divorce. "How long is your husband's furlough?" asked the judge.

"Seven inches!" the Italian girl replied.

"I mean, how long does he get off?"

"Just long enough for a cigarette and a cup of coffee!"

* * *

Private Iverson was trying to get a discharge from the army, so he pretended he was going blind. The doctor examining him believed he was faking and at a prearranged signal had the voluptuous nurse strip off her blouse.

"What do you see?" asked the doctor.

"Not a thing," said the soldier. "Just a blur!"

"Your eyes may not be much good, son," said the M.D., "but your pecker is pointing straight to Fort Dix."

* * *

Cowen arrived in his North Dakota home on furlough. He kissed his wife and then declared, "Honey, get your sweeping done around the house, because for the next two weeks you're not going to see anything but the ceiling!"

Staff Sergeant Dumbrowski wrote to his wife from France. "Gee, all the women around the base are gold diggers."

And the wife quickly wired him, "Don't pay them any more than twenty dollars. That's all I'm getting here!"

* * *

Phillips, Sutter, and Nichols, three World War II vets, met at an American Legion convention and began bragging about their exploits. Phillips told about the time he was on the battlefield in a jeep and had it shot out from under him so that he had to continue by foot.

Sutter told how he had a tank shot out from under him and had to continue by foot.

Then Nichols told how he had a WAC shot out from under him and had to continue by hand!

* * *

A horny marine, Sergeant Ellis,
With esprit de corps much too zealous
　　Drilled his dong to stand stiff
　　At the whiff of a quiff
While his bottom blew "Semper Fidelis."

* * *

After three years in Vietnam, Colonel Andersen returned home to his wife. Having been accustomed to low-class floozies in Saigon, he was disappointed to find his wife with a heavy bush that she would not shave.

She said that the hairy growth kept her warm in winter, and that shaving her crotch was immodest and that she didn't want to look like a cheap whore. Nothing Andersen could do would change her mind.

Several weeks later, coming home after a night of drinking with the boys, Andersen grabbed his wife, threw her on the bed, and tied her arms and legs to the bedposts. Then, with his electric razor, he began to shave off her pubic hair.

She begged him to stop. She pleaded. She cried, "If you do this, you'll be sorry the rest of your life."

But the colonel wouldn't listen. When Andersen had finished and blew away the loose hair, he found neatly tattooed underneath:

KILROY WAS HERE.

* * *

Private First Class Schreiber and his girl burst in on the justice of the peace and told them that they wanted to be married immediately. "Sorry," said the justice, "but even a special license would take two days."

"Eh, look," said the GI, "couldn't you say a few words just to tide us over the weekend?"

* * *

A squad of soldiers on maneuvers in the Tennessee hills stumbled on a girl bent over a washtub scrubbing clothes. One of the soldiers crept up behind the girl and had intercourse with her. She went right on washing. Another soldier diddled her, then several more.

After they all left, an old mule ambled over for his turn. The girl kept on washing. But as the mule was about done, she said, "Will the last gentleman please leave his name and address!"

* * *

There was a young farm girl named Bunny
    Whose kisses were sweeter than honey;
      And the GIs galore
      Would line up at her door
    To take turns in paying her money.

* * *

161

A soldier and a sailor were killed in action at the same moment and reached the pearly gates at exactly the same time. As Saint Peter gave them angelic wings, he warned, "One unclean or unkind thought will cause these feathery appendages to drop off, so be careful."

A few minutes later, a beautiful, well-built female angel swished by. Immediately, the soldier's wings dropped off. As he bent over to pick them up, the sailor's wings also fell.

Every day while he was away, Corporal Cusick's sweetheart sent him a naked photo of herself, legs wide open in straddle beaver style, with a note that said, "This is how I'll stay until you return."

And he never once thought to ask, "Who's taking those pictures?"

* * *

Wallace and Toomey were being flown home after several months at a remote Alaska outpost.

"Do you know what's the first thing I'm gonna do when we land?" asked Wallace.

"That depends," said Toomey, "on whether you see your wife before I do!"

* * *

BARRACK BAG

A polite name for the platoon poontang

* * *

Did you hear about the soldier who was supposed to police the barracks but ended up in the guardhouse for putting WACs on the floor?

* * *

Private Henderson, a huge black from Mississippi, complained of dizziness and was sent to the base hospital. Late in the afternoon, the doctor got around to his case and wrote on the pad as treatment, "Give this man an enema."

The day nurse, just before he went off, came in, read the instructions, and proceeded to carry them out.

Half an hour later, an orderly came in, saw the instructions not yet crossed out, and gave the patient a second enema.

The night nurse came on within an hour, found the doctor's memorandum, and gave still a third enema to the frightened soldier.

"Man, this gotta stop!" the black man said to himself. Exhausted as he was, Henderson locked the door and pulled a couple of chairs over in front of it. Then he got back into bed and began to doze off.

Suddenly, there was a sharp knocking on the door. A voice said, "Open up! Let me in!"

Henderson raised his head from the bed. "Who is you?" His voice quavered. "Friend or enema?"

* * *

165

Benton was sitting in a little off-base cocktail lounge shooting the breeze with the bartender.

"Things at the camp are great. We even got us a gorgeous blonde in our barracks."

"What!" said the bartender. "You must be kidding. Is she a WAC?"

"No," said the soldier. "She's just one of the boys. Matter of fact, she helps around the joint. We bring her food from the mess, and she sleeps in the barracks. She even takes showers where we do."

"Wow!" said the barkeep. "How does she get away with it?"

"No problem." The GI winked. "Who's gonna snitch?"

* * *

Did you hear about the nearsighted turtle that had a nervous breakdown?

She fell in love with an army helmet.

* * *

There was a WAC sergeant named Nellie
Whose breasts could be joggled like jelly.
    They could tie in a knot
    Or reach you know what
Or even swat flies on her belly.

* * *

At an overseas army base, Colonel Duncan was lecturing her newly arrived WAC platoon on proper behavior of service women. After much advice on what to do and what not to do in uniform, she ended by saying:

"So remember, if you're going to do anything that will disgrace your uniform, take it off."

* * *

Did you hear about the runaway army truck that slammed into the hen house?

You should have seen all the chickens hit.

* * *

Yinkey was sitting in the camp hospital waiting to see the doctor. He overheard some other GIs complaining about the medical treatment. One guy mentioned that his buddy had his ear cut off by a medico because he had an ear infection.

A second soldier mentioned that his buddy had his toe cut off because he had ptomaine poisoning. Just then, Yinkey jumped up and started to leave.

"Where you goin'? What's the hurry?"

"This is no place for me," answered the soldier. "I've been suffering from prickly heat!"

* * *

Belding, an obnoxious used-car dealer, was a colonel in the army reserves. During a summer training tour, he took sick and was hospitalized in the officer's ward. At the hospital, he "pulled rank," threw his weight around, and generally harassed the staff.

One day, Private Eskridge, on duty in the hospital, recognized Belding as the man who had sold him a lemon. He dressed himself up in the white apparel of a surgeon. Eskridge glanced at the colonel's chart and ordered the patient to get up on his hands and knees to receive a rectal thermometer. "I've got to leave for an urgent case now," said the GI, "but don't you move 'til I come back."

Thirty minutes later, a nurse walking through the ward stopped short at Belding's bedside.

"Colonel," she exclaimed, "what are you doing?"

"Taking my temperature," he growled. "Anything wrong with that?"

"But, colonel," gasped the nurse, "with a daffodil?"

Major Moss got transferred to a new base and after a few weeks got horny. He went to the C.O. "Sir, may I have a weekend pass. I could really use a little action."

"I wish I could give you a pass, but I have orders to keep everyone on the base."

"But, sir, I'm really in big need."

"Sorry. I suggest you go see Sergeant Hollister."

"I don't go for that stuff!" said Moss, leaving the office. Three weeks later, the major returned to the C.O.'s office. "Sir, I'm losing my mind! Could I go into town just for tonight? I promise I'll be back in the morning?"

"Like I said, I can't let anyone leave the base. Now I told you that you could go see Sergeant Hollister."

"And I told you, I don't go for that stuff!"

Nine weeks later, he returned. "Sir, I think I'm gonna crack up. I've gotta get some action."

"I told you that you could go see Sergeant Hollister."

"All right, I'll go see Hollister."

"OK, tonight you meet me here at eight o'clock with six guys."

"What in the hell do I need six guys for?"

"To hold down Sergeant Hollister—he don't go for that stuff, either!"

170

* * *

Campbell came home after a year of overseas duty and found his wife sick. He took her to the doctor, who told him confidentially that his wife was pregnant.

"That's impossible," snarled the GI. "I've been away for over a year!"

"We've had cases like this before," replied the M.D. "We call it grudge pregnancy. You see, someone had it in for you!"

* * *

Miss Kazinski, a pretty barmaid, complained to the doctor that she felt a burning sensation when she went to the bathroom. "You've got P.D.," he said.

"What's that?" she asked.

"Why that's a private disease," answered the doctor.

"That louse!" the Polish girl shouted. "He told me he was a lieutenant."

* * *

There was a young miss from Cape Cod
    Who at soldiers would not even nod.
        But she tripped in a ditch,
        And some son of a bitch
    Of a corporal raped her, by God!

* * *

"Why was there such an increase in the birth rate during the war?"

" 'Cause the men were scared stiff, and the women took advantage of it."

* * *

SERVICEMAN'S SONNET

The birds do it;
The bees do it;
The little bats do it,
So he joined the air force.

* * *

SIGN ON WOMEN'S ARMY BARRACKS

If We Had Nuts Instead of Cracks,
We'd Be GIs Instead of WACs.

172

Spicy Sparklers

Regent sat in the doctor's office. "What can I do for you?" asked the M.D.

"I suffer from premature ejaculation."

"When does this occur?"

"Between 'Hello' and 'What's your sign'?"

* * *

"Doctors now say that sex is good for relieving arthritis symptoms," said Blair to his girl friend.

"But you don't have arthritis," she replied.

"Haven't you heard of preventive medicine?"

173

* * *

What do you call a nurse with sore knees?

The head nurse.

* * *

SALESMAN'S SONG

She was only the trailer manufacturer's daughter, but you could make her connection without a hitch.

* * *

Late one night in a Bel Air estate, the butler was diddling the pretty new maid on the kitchen table. They were going at it hot and heavy when suddenly he began to scream like a maniac.

"Say, when you come, you really do come," said the girl.

"Like hell I do," yelled the butler. "I got my balls caught in the drawer."

* * *

Doctor (Taking up his stethoscope): Big breaths.

Myrna: Yeth, and I'm not thixteen yet.

* * *

What's smaller than a teeny-weeny flea?
A flea's teeny weeny.

* * *

Did you hear about the new pill out
now just for masochists?
It brings slow-slow relief.

* * *

Masochist (Pleading): Beat me! Beat me!
Sadist (Sneering):   No!

* * *

"Poor Pandora."
"What happened?"
"Her box wore out!"

* * *

What is the difference between a pregnant woman and a light bulb?
You can unscrew a light bulb.

* * *

Legs are a girl's best friend, but even
the best of friends must soon part.

* * *

The night before the battle of Bunker Hill, Ethan and John, two Massachusetts militiamen, sat beside their fire. "Ethan," said John, "did you hear the one about the two whores—"

"Wait a minute!" interrupted Ethan. "Why do all your stories have to be about whores?"

"They don't," said John. "This one could be about beautiful ladies."

"All right," said Ethan. "Tell it that way, then."

"Okay. These two beautiful ladies were working in a whore house . . ."

* * *

MUZZLE

French chastity belt

* * *

Did you hear about the new pill called Transpan?

It's half tranquilizer and half Spanish fly—makes you want it bad as hell, but if you don't get any, you don't give a damn.

* * *

What is sixteen inches long, white, and hard?

Nothing.

* * *

There was a young lady from Sydney
Who could take it right up to her kidney.
But a man from Quebec
Shoved it up to her neck.
He had a long one, now didn't he?

* * *

Why is a woman like peanut butter?
Both have to be spread to be eaten.

* * *

Garner invited Drusilla to his apartment for dinner. He had big bedroom plans in mind, but not being the bold, brash type, he wondered how to broach the subject. When they finished their meal and were sitting on the sofa, he came up with an idea. Filling both their glasses with a good brandy, he raised his drink in a toast.

"Bottom's up!" he declared. "Or any other position that appeals to you."

* * *

Mrs. Crawford walked into Bazinski's bakery. When the owner did not appear, she wandered to the back and found him using his upper plate to decorate the cookies. The woman watched in shock and then gasped. "I thought you have a tool for that!"

"No," said the Polack. "That's for making the doughnuts."

What is the smallest thing in the world?
A nit on the nut of a gnat.

* * *

NAUGHTY NURSERY RHYME

Little Boy Blue
Lay down in the corn
While Little Red Riding Hood
Blew his horn

* * *

How can you tell if a clam is male or female?

You take and smash it against the wall. If it screams, "Ouch, my balls!" it's a guy.

* * *

A foot was talking to a penis. "I really have a rotten life," said the foot. "All my owner does is stick me in this smelly shoe and make me walk around on it all day."

"I have a worse life than you," said the penis. "They stick me in this dark cave every day and make me do push-ups until I throw up."

* * *

Did you hear about the fellow who went bald from doing U-turns under the sheets?

*   *   *

Why can't Frankenstein have any kids?
'Cause his nuts are in his neck.

*   *   *

What do you get if you cross an elephant with a hooker?
A very nice girl who does it for peanuts . . .
And never forgets a friend.

*   *   *

Waitress: You got to be kiddin'? After I've been standing on my feet all day?

Truck Driver: Well, honey, I ain't asking you to do it standing up!

*   *   *

AIRCRAFT CARRIER

A stewardess with VD

*   *   *

181

Noreen, a pretty Vegas showgirl, started analysis. On her first visit, the shrink began spouting a lot of sexual terms. "Wait a minute," she interrupted. "What's a phallic symbol?"

"A phallic symbol," explained the doctor, "represents the phallus."

"Okay," said Noreen. "What's a phallus?"

"I guess," said the analyst, "the best way to explain it is to show you." He stood up, unzipped his fly, and took out his pecker.

"This, young lady, is a phallus."

"Oh-h-h!" said the showgirl. "You mean it's like a prick, only smaller."

Maisie suffered from being nearsighted, a malady she felt prevented her from having long-term relationships. When she met Abner, Maisie determined to hide her nearsightedness from him. One day, she hid a gold brooch in a small clump of bushes. That night, while she and Abner were making love under a tree two hundred yards away, she suddenly stopped. "What's the matter?" cried Abner.

"Look, isn't that a gold brooch over there in those bushes?" said the girl.

"I couldn't see a brooch as far away as that!"

"I'll get it for you," she said, and started off. Then Maisie tripped and fell over a cow.

* * *

Psychiatrist: Did your folks ever catch you masturbating?
Patient: No!
Psychiatrist: Really? You must have had a good hiding place.

* * *

If all the girls in the world were blades of grass, what would all the boys be?
Grasshoppers.

* * *

A nice little number named Nancy
Got all likkered up and romancy.
    A fellow named Anson
    Did all the romancin',
So she knew it was Anson her pantsy.

* * *

"Hello," said the woman's voice over the phone. "Are you Harry?"

"No," said the fellow, "but I'm not exactly bald, either."

* * *

NEW FIRST-AID BOOKLET

"How To Administer Mouth to Mouth Resuscitation without Becoming Emotionally Involved"

* * *

How many calories in sex?
None if you don't eat it.

* * *

What is a Greek gentleman?
One who will take a girl out three times before he approaches her brother.

* * *

What's the difference between a well-stacked blonde in the daytime and the same dame in the nighttime?

In the daytime, she's fair and buxom.

* * *

A lifeguard in Atlantic City heard a swimmer shouting in a deep bass voice, "Help! Sharks! For God's sake, help!"

Then, in a high-pitched falsetto: "Too late! Too late!"

* * *

Did you hear about the new birth control method called Sulfa Denial.

It's a derivative of No-acetol.

* * *

DAFFY DITTY

She was only a telegrapher's daughter
But she didit . . . didit . . . didit.

* * *

What did Adam do when he saw that he and Eve were different?

He split the difference.

* * *

On an Amtrak to San Diego, Emily and Anabel were discussing clothes while Morrison across the aisle pretended to be asleep.

"The cost of clothes today is impossible," said Emily.

"Why not do what I do, darlin'," suggested Anabel. "Get yourself a guy on the side. He'll give you five hundred dollars a month for spending money. Your husband'd never do that."

"But what if I can't get a guy with five hundred?"

"Then take two with two fifty each."

Morrison spoke up, "Listen, girls, I'm goin' to sleep now. Wake me up when you get down to twenty bucks."

* * *

What's a gentleman?

A guy who puts at least half his weight on his elbows.

NEWS ITEM

Science has proved that upon retiring for the night, the average person changes position at least a dozen times. Then there are those who prefer normal sex!

* * *

"Hey, did you hear they arrested Arnie for dating some teenage virgin?"

"No kidding? What was the charge?"

"Breaking and entering."

* * *

Giovanni's son came home from college and said, "Pop, here's a riddle for you. What is it that's hard and long and leaks?"

"Is that the dirty things they teach-a you in school!" exclaimed the old Italian.

"Don't get excited, pop! It's a fountain pen!"

The next night, Giovanni was invited to a church dinner. Just after the dessert, he said, "I have-a da riddle. What's-a hard and a long and leaks?"

The women gasped and turned their heads away. "Don't get excited, ladies!" said Giovanni. "It ain't-a prick. It's a fountain pen!"

* * *

There once was a Genie
With a ten-foot weenie
　　Who showed it to the girl next
door.
She thought it was a snake
And hit it with a rake
　　And now it's only five foot four.

Who's the bravest man in the world?

The peanut vendor. He whistles while his nuts are burning.

* * *

Did you hear about the guy with five pricks?

His pants fit him like a glove.

* * *

When Mohambi, the president of a new African country, visited Moscow, he watched a game of Russian roulette being played by members of the diplomatic corps. A player put the barrel of a pistol to his head and pulled the trigger. One of the six chambers contained a real bullet.

Six months later, the Russian diplomat was visiting the African nation.

"We would like to show you our version of roulette," said Mohambi. "We call this African roulette."

"How do you play it?"

The president pointed to six buxom black females sitting in a circle. "Any of these girls will give you a blow job."

"Where is the roulette part? Where is the jeopardy?" asked the red diplomat.

"Well," said the African, "one of the girls is a cannibal!"

189

BEAUTY CONTEST

A show where they judge young ladies on looks, talent, and poise, then place a crown on the one with the biggest tits.

* * *

Dwayne and Maude were embracing in the back seat of his car out on lovers lane. "H-m-m, you're crushing me," moaned Maude.

"I could squeeze ya till you break!" he said passionately.

So he gave her a tight hug, and sure enough, he felt her crack.

* * *

The Chicago hotel elevator operator called, "Floors, please!"

Armstrong, standing in back of the car, called out, "Ballroom, please!"

"Oh, I'm sorry," said the cute blonde in front of him. "I didn't realize I was crowding you."

* * *

What is the cure for the Hawaiian disease lackanookie?

Slipadictomy.

* * *

On a Kansas city street corner, an inquiring reporter stopped a middle-aged woman. "Do you believe in strict punishment for sex offenders?"

"Yes, I suppose so," she smiled. "Unless the rape occurred in self-defense."

* * *

What do they call the operation for appendicitis?

Appendectomy.

What do they call the operation for tonsillitis?

Tonsillectomy.

What do they call a female sex-change operation?

Addadictomy.

* * *

What has eighteen legs and a vagina?
The Supreme Court.

* * *

ECOLOGY BUMPER STICKER

Eat a beaver—save a tree.

* * *

Miss Fernandez entered the New York subway and waited for the uptown local. Suddenly, a weirdo flung open his trench coat to expose himself. "Please, not tonight!" she exclaimed. "I've got a headache!"

"How'd you like Hawaii?"

"Great. The girls wear nothing but grass skirts—what a place to hit the hay!"

* * *

Caroline, taking the train to Washington, had a zipper bag beside her with a lunch in it packed by her mother. She fell asleep, and Dudley, a Georgetown senior, pushed the lunch bag out of the way and sat down beside her. He, too, fell asleep.

Caroline dreamt that she was hungry, unzipped the bag in her sleep, and began eating her lunch.

"Oh, goody!" she cried, still asleep. "Two hard-boiled eggs and the neck of a chicken!"

* * *

Jenkins, a black steelworker, arrived at work one morning and was greeted by his buddy, Belson. "Hey, man," he said, "you looks bad! Is you sick or somethin'?"

"I feels fine," retorted Jenkins.

"You may feel OK, but you looks bad!"

Ten minutes later, the foreman told Jenkins he didn't look too well, but he insisted that he felt fine.

After several workmen commented on

his sickly appearance, Jenkins took the afternoon off to get medical assistance. He went to Dr. Dandridge, who had just opened his "office" in Harlem. Jenkins entered the empty waiting room and found a black doctor seated behind a battered old wooden desk. "What seems to be your problem, my man?" asked the M.D."

"Well, all my friends says I looks bad—but I feels good!"

Dandridge reached down into a desk drawer and remarked, "You is in luck, 'cause I just got a new book o' syndromes, and we can look that up. Now let me see here. 'Looks bad, feels bad.' That ain't right. 'Looks good, feels bad.' No, that ain't it. Aha! Here it is. "Looks bad, feels good.' "

"Okay," exclaimed Jenkins. "C'mon, give it to me straight. What's the problem?"

"I don't know how to tell this to you," said the medical man, "but when you looks bad and you feels good, it means you is a vagina!"

* * *

SILLY SONG

She was only a photographer's daughter, but she knew how to enlarge it.

* * *

195

Remember: When you say *oragenital-ism*, you've said a mouthful!

* * *

Why is a sun-tanned girl like a roast chicken?
Because the white parts are the best.

* * *

And don't ever forget:
The point of a joke is like a good piece of tail—it's no good if you don't get it!

WILDE ON WILDE

I love humor. I've spent over 30 years studying, analyzing, researching, teaching, performing, and writing it. The fascination started in Jersey City where I was born in 1928. As a kid during the Depression I had to scratch hard to make a buck, and making jokes was a way of life.

After a two-year stint in the Marine Corps, where I found I could make leathernecks laugh, I worked my way through the University of Miami, Florida, doing a comedy act at the hotels. After graduating, I entertained in night-clubs and theaters around the U.S. I got to play Vegas and Tahoe and the other big-time spots being the "supporting" comedian for Ann-Margret, Debbie Reynolds, Pat Boone, and many others.

I've done acting roles on *The Mary Tyler Moore Show, Rhoda, Sanford & Son* and other sitcoms, performed on Carson, Griffin, Douglas and did a bunch of TV commercials.

This is my 32nd joke book. I'm also proud of the two serious works I've done on comedy technique: *The Great Comedians Talk About Comedy* and *How the Great Comedy Writers Create Laughter*. Both books have been called "definitive" works on the subject.

My books have sold over 7,000,000 copies, which makes them the biggest-selling humor series in publishing history. And while I'm blowing my own horn here, the best thing I ever did was to marry Maryruth Poulos, a really talented writer from Wyoming.